'Terrific ... Britai[n] [is] [...] [lig]hted with myth and mystery [...] [...] [conti]nents and [Rees] proves it by [...] [...] [...]ing stories.'
– *Sunday Times*, **Best Books of the Year, 2020**

'Unexpected and fascinating.'
– **Melissa Harrison, author of** *The Stubborn Light of Things*

'Edgeland wanderers and psychogeographers will find a wealth of shabby but otherworldly relics of abandonment ... evoking the most eerie of locations, this book will appeal to ley hunters, psychic questers, urban explorers, psychogeographers and all edgeland wanderers.'
– *Fortean Times*

'Rees finds soul in these soulless locations, charting stories and encounters as rich as those found among rolling hills and chocolate box villages. A delight.'
– *The New European*

'Should be required reading in every motorway service station coffee shop up and down this land.'
– *The Psychogeographic Review*

'You should read this book. It will make you stay up too late, laugh out loud, and then freak yourself out looking out of the window at the haunted-looking binbag blowing past Carpet Right in the dead of night.'
– **Michael Smith, author of** *Unreal City*

UNOFFICIAL
BRITAIN

UNOFFICIAL BRITAIN

BRITAIN

JOURNEYS

THROUGH

UNEXPECTED

PLACES

GARETH E. REES

Elliott&Thompson

First published 2020 by
Elliott and Thompson Limited
2 John Street
London WC1N 2ES
www.eandtbooks.com

This paperback edition published in 2021

ISBN: 978-1-78396-596-0

Permissions:
Page 22: Extract from 'Pylon' by Annie Muir, reproduced with permission
(http://time41poem.WordPress.com); page 154: Extract from *Flood Drain* by
Tom Chivers (Annexe Press, 2014), reproduced with permission; page 206:
Extract from 'A Sentence' by Dan Duggan, published in *Luxury of the
Dispossessed* (Influx Press, 2015), reproduced with permission.

Pictures:
Page 15: 'Twilight of the Gods' by Maxim Griffin; page 89: 'The Ghost Box'
by Mark Hollis.

All other photos by Gareth E. Rees.

9 8 7 6 5 4 3 2 1

A catalogue record for this book is available from
the British Library.

Cover design by Jack Smyth
Typesetting by Marie Doherty
Printed in the UK by TJ Books Ltd

FSC
www.fsc.org
MIX
Paper from
responsible sources
FSC® C013056

To my daughters, Isis and Venus

'Everything has beauty, but not everyone sees it.'
– CONFUCIUS

CONTENTS

INTRODUCTION

THE MAGIC, MYTHOLOGY AND FOLKLORE OF URBAN SPACE

After a long trudge over a misty moor, you arrive at the crest of a hill and pause for breath by an oak tree. Initials have been etched into the bark by others who have stood here. Lovers. Friends. Mourners. Your eye follows a drystone wall down to the valley below, where a river meanders through a meadow; a Civil War battle took place there, one so bloody that the water ran red for a week. You smell smoke. Hear the crackle of burning wood. A crow flies out from the spire of a derelict church just visible above the trees. Bells begin to toll but you know there have been no bells in that church tower for decades. With a shiver, you descend through a holloway worn by generations of feet, hooves and cartwheels. Shafts of light glance off glistering spiderwebs. It grows cold and you don't know why. But you've heard stories about this path: the murderer who fled along it from a nearby village then vanished into thin air; the stagecoach crash that killed two lovers whose voices are sometimes heard in the wind; the knoll on which it is said a witch's house once stood, where now no flowers grow. On reaching the village, you stop outside its pub, where a mummified cat is displayed above the door and a memorial plaque tells of the man who propped up the bar each night and sang old songs until his forearms wore grooves into the wood. Streamers dangle from street lamps, remnants of May

Day festivities. You stand on the cobbled street, revelling in Merrie Olde England.

This romanticised folkloric version of Britain belongs to a time before the Industrial Revolution, when the majority of people lived and worked in the countryside. We see glimpses of it when we venture down country lanes, through woods and vales, to villages with Tudor houses, Norman churches and pretty greens. It is embedded in our collective memory in the form of pastoral paintings, poetry, songs and stories. This pre-industrial age is often sentimentalised as a purer, more magical epoch of wonder and mystery, its landscape unspoiled and picturesque. Of course, if you had been alive at the time, it would simply have been *the everyday*; you would not have considered yourself to be living in some sublime English Eden. On the contrary, life could be brutish. Winter was tough. Homes were dirty. Work was back-breaking. Murder and rape often went undetected and unpunished. Poverty was common. There were outbreaks of disease, war and famine.

Humans have always harboured anxieties about the state of the world and the threats we face, both in this life and in whatever comes after. Before the majority could read or afford books, the primary medium for expressing these fears, ideals and superstitions was through oral storytelling. Local lore sprang from numerous, nebulous sources: rumours that grew and mutated; collective memories; political propaganda; tales told to keep children from danger; tragic events; wrongful executions; unsolved murders; explanations for natural phenomena and topographic curiosities; aftershocks of plague, war and conflict. They all originated in real events and landscapes but persisted through the ages as fiction – nursery rhymes, aphorisms, myths and legends of witches, boggarts, phantom dogs that roam the hills, and ghosts of grieving widows and long-dead soldiers. These stories are expressed in dances, festivals and rituals or through totems such as Sheela-na-gigs, foliate heads and gargoyles. They're encoded in the names of lanes and alleys, woodlands and caves, ancient wells and stones – places that have seen so many cycles of birth and death, love and grief, hope and regret that they cannot help but be deeply storied.

But wonderful though these places are, most of us today don't live in picture-postcard villages with thatched roofs, medieval inns and ancient customs, and there is a danger in fetishising that past as a halcyon world that has since been contaminated by technological progress, urbanisation and immigration. The past was not a utopia and a 'pure' Britain has never existed in any era. The Romans, Angles, Saxons, Jutes, Danes and Normans left traces of their gods, ghosts and demons well before the end of the Middle Ages, just as African, Caribbean, Indian, Eastern European and Middle Eastern immigrants have endowed us with their traditions, music and cuisine since the days of Empire. Our culture is in constant development. The story never stops.

The industrial revolution tore up much of 'Merrie Olde England'. People migrated in huge numbers to cities and big towns to work in factories. Mining, quarrying and new

infrastructure transformed the topography. Rivers were canalised. Railways cut through the countryside, bringing noise
and pollution, allowing for travel so fast it changed our con-
cepts of time and distance. We replaced the circadian rhythms
of nature with the rhythms of machinery, clocks and production deadlines. Great iron bridges spanned gorges and valleys.
Ships brought cargo to bustling docklands from all parts of
the Empire. Chimneys thrust into the skyline. Cities sprawled
outward, consuming marshes, farms and villages. New urban
landscapes presented us with new threats, new fears, new
hopes, and new avenues for the imagination. Jack the Ripper
and Spring Heeled Jack terrorised the smog-shrouded streets
of London. Body snatchers skulked in mass cemeteries. New
photographic technology captured 'proof' of ghosts and fairies, while early electronic devices detected spirit voices in the
ether. As science clashed with superstition, Victorian anxieties
found expression in Jekyll and Hyde dichotomies, vampires
with sexually transmitted infections, wars against superior alien
technologies, and apocalyptic flood scenarios. New mythical
narratives were born in this post-industrial age, which today
we take for granted.

Of course, many of the traditions of rural England died
during the seismic social shifts of the industrial revolution.
Communities lost their generational continuity. Urban life
detached people from their connection to the land, and to the
seasons. Scientific enlightenment challenged superstitions and
cast electric light into the shadowy corners where ghosts and

demons used to hide. Many bemoaned the ugliness, pollution and overcrowding of the modern world: human beings hemmed into factories and slums, their children sick and malnourished. But as generations grew up in this environment, they knew only brick and iron, gaslit streets, steam engines and factories. This was the backdrop to their lives and loves, their dreams and nightmares. But when they died, they too left their ghosts behind, and the urban environment became as endowed with melancholy, sentimentality and nostalgia as the rural world it had superseded. Today we instinctively see beauty in an old mill, iron bridge or viaduct. It is easy to feel sentimental at the sight of chimney stacks silhouetted on a jumble of slate roofs. We don't think there's anything incongruous about an eerie tale set by a foggy canal, a defunct railway line or an abandoned mine shaft. It wouldn't surprise us at all to feel haunted inside a Victorian terraced house. These sites have a powerful resonance, saturated as they are with the many events that have occurred there. We can feel the sadness in their decay and can easily imagine the stories of their departed inhabitants.

The First World War shattered the old world and heralded a new technological era. Battles were fought with machine guns, chemical weapons, tanks and planes. Cinema brought horror and science fiction to big screens. The BBC beamed radio transmissions into homes. The Second World War took the country to the brink of annihilation. The Blitz destroyed swathes of buildings in our cities and created spaces for fresh architectural visions in the form of housing estates, tower blocks and shopping centres. The age of the automobile brought motorways, car parks, roundabouts and retail parks. Flyovers cut through residential areas. Ring roads, link roads and urban motorways carved up cities and split communities. Victorian slums were demolished. Bypasses sliced through the country-side. Concrete, glass and steel changed the colours, shapes and textures of the cityscape. The establishment of the NHS saw many hospitals built or extended. Vapour trails criss-crossed the sky as airports expanded. Derelict docks were redeveloped to become homes, leisure facilities, retail spaces and business premises. The production of coal, iron and steel gave way to the manufacture of white goods, convenience foods and electronics. To keep track with demand, electricity pylons ranged ever more widely across the landscape. Substations buzzed at the edges of towns. Nuclear power stations rose up on the coastline. The skyline bristled with masts for radio, TV and mobile phones.

With these changes came new dangers and anxieties: of road accidents, electrocutions, cancer, pollution, environmental catas-trophe and nuclear attack. These found additional expression in new media forms. Warnings were disseminated in public informa-tion films. Imaginings of disaster were manifested in TV dramas such as *Doctor Who*, *The Day of the Triffids* and *Threads*. Graffiti and street art told parallel stories in the shadows of concrete and steel. Disaffection in the suburbs became the stuff of punk and new wave. Drum 'n' bass, hip-hop and grime were transmitted from industrial estates and tower blocks. Conspiracy websites spread rumours across the limitless expanse of cyberspace, bringing dreams and nightmares to high-powered computers in the palms of our hands.

It is in this urban landscape, shaped by the second half of the twentieth century, that over 80 per cent of us live. Many people believe that much has been lost in the process. Identikit hotels, chain stores and car parks have eroded our sense of place. Zones of transit such as airports, railway stations and motorways make you feel as if you could be anywhere in the country, detached from local culture. Central heating, air conditioning and the supply of mass-produced goods flown in from around the world have severed our connection to the seasons. There are fewer community hubs where people can make friends and share stories. Screens – large and small – absorb our attention and detach us from what's happening around us. The artefacts of consumerism have pervaded every aspect of modern life, from shopping malls and supermarkets to billboards on the streets and advertising jingles on the airwaves.

All of this may be true, but to proclaim that there is no longer any myth, mystery or beauty in our culture diminishes our everyday lived experience and underestimates the creative capacity of our minds. Our brains have essentially remained unchanged since the Stone Age. We have the same instinct to seek patterns in the chaos. We still yearn to make sense of the mystery of existence. We still tell stories to help us process the world. We still have an emotional attachment to places and objects. These impulses have not died beneath the concrete and tarmac of the modern world, any more than they did beneath the iron and brick of the industrial revolution. If you look closely enough, all landscapes can be fascinating and any object, no matter what its material, can be freighted with meaning. A Styrofoam chip sent whirling across a motorway by the cough of a truck exhaust can be as compelling as an oak leaf spinning in the breeze above a brook – they both ripple with the elements of the universe. They can tell a story or trigger an emotion, which is why it is possible to feel as much wonder and fear in a car park, power station, underpass or waste ground as you can in a ruined castle or dark spooky wood. In modern terms – they *are* the ruined castle and the dark spooky wood, where monsters and ghouls may lurk.

We have existed for over seventy years in a world of motor-ways, roundabouts, high-rises, cooling towers, malls and pylons. They are part of a century that is already way behind us, slipping quickly into history. The structures we think of as 'modern' are in fact analogue relics of a bygone era before digital technol-ogy, mobile phones and the internet. Generations have lived and died among them, played among them, attached memories to them. If the railway bridges, viaducts, gasometers, mills and docks of the nineteenth century can be storied, romanticised and mythologised then so too can the incursions of the late twen-tieth century. They have been around long enough to become layered with stories as they gradually decay. Once-visionary tower blocks are crumbling. Multistorey car parks have become as weathered and worn as castles. Underpasses are the dark haunts of nocturnal opportunists. Motorways are steeped in blood, scarred by loss and memories of journeys past. Some of these structures have become pariahs: the source of rumours; scapegoats for social problems; no-go areas that parents warn their children about. But however mundane or brutal they might be, these are places we remember, in which our daily dramas unfold. The crash of scrap metal, the hum of an overhead power line or the whoosh of tyres on tarmac can take a seventy-year-old back to her childhood as easily as the song of a skylark. Inside each of us is a rich anthology of tiny, yet meaningful moments, played out in locations that have acquired dramatic qualities as a result – the hospital, the shopping centre, the service station, the cul-de-sac, the tumbledown wasteland.

The stories of previous epochs haven't disappeared either, even when buildings have been demolished and their inhabitants are long dead. They can be found in old mine shafts and cursed wells beneath housing developments, Roman ruins beneath service stations and Victorian houses trapped within industrial sprawls. They're in the roundabouts that have replaced historical crossroads, the car parks built on former cemeteries, and the steel factories operating where monasteries once stood. They're in the artworks, both sanctioned and illegal, that celebrate a location's history. They're in the memories passed down through generations. They're in the tales we tell. As the geographer Doreen Massey once said, space 'is always in the process of being made. It is never finished; never closed. Perhaps we could imagine space as a simultaneity of stories-so-far.' That narrative constantly evolves. Flyovers that once destroyed urban communities have themselves come to harbour new communities of artists, outcasts and ravers with their own myths and legends. Long-reviled transmission masts, pylons and chimneys have become beloved landmarks that anchor us to a place. Suburban housing estates that once seemed so lacking in history have become ingrained with tragic events, haunted by their own kinds of ghosts.

In 2014, I set up the website Unofficial Britain as a platform for writing, art and film that tell stories about overlooked modern landscapes. My contributors and I are fascinated by urban legends, uncanny events, contemporary folklore, and cryptozoological beasts. We explore alternative histories. We share unreliable memories. We walk through familiar places, such as car parks, bus stops, amusement arcades and promenades, and find that the closer we look, the stranger these places become. We have explored the mythology of the Thamesmead social housing development; the lost lido of Dunbar; a waterway built by Sir Francis Drake in a Plymouth retail park; a bullet-riddled ghost village on Salisbury Plain; recollections of a tenement block in 1970s Whitechapel; the meaning of white paint spills in public places; and the melancholy phenomenon of abandoned toys.

In this book I continue the journey, visiting modern urban spaces that are neglected, dismissed or edited out of the official ꞌꞌre of Britain. They are not prime locations on the cultural ꞌꞌot the expected destinations for a traveller. They're picturesque or unusual examples of their kind, nor are they likely to be featured on Atlas Obscura-style lists of weird places and hidden wonders. These are quotidian spaces with which we are all familiar, and yet they have the capacity to contain mystery, tragedy and even beauty. They tell a different story of the urban landscape, one that is subjective, multifarious and ever-changing. They include structures, towns and cities that resonate with my own history, and which have contributed to my personal mythos. You'll discover a haunted electricity pylon on a Yorkshire bypass, druidic roundabouts in Scotland, fairies under a Wirral motorway, a cursed wall in a Welsh steelworks, a 'cat man' in a Clydeside industrial estate, a shed of brains in a South London hospital, phantoms in multistorey car parks, ghosts in a Lincolnshire council estate, the so-called 'Bermuda Triangle' of the M6, and religious iconography in a service station chain hotel. These are the first shoots of future folklore emerging from an urban Britain that might look soulless and secular but under the surface remains very strange indeed, rippled with weird undercurrents. The backdrop to these stories might have changed since the days of Merrie Olde England but that impulse to make sense of the world through our imaginations remains as powerful as ever.

Welcome to Unofficial Britain.

1

IN WORSHIP
OF THE HUM

THE STRANGE RELIGION
OF ELECTRICITY PYLONS

My first memories. Or rather, not the first, but those fragments which have survived the pressure of time and become bright diamonds in the mind. It's 1979. I'm six years old and I'm on the way home from Oxgang Primary in the town of Kirkintilloch on the outskirts of Glasgow. I don't remember why I am walking alone. All I recall is the pavement, black with silver flecks, and the drain by the kerb, over which I stand with a bunch of my drawings, which the teacher has told me to take home. I don't want to take them home. They're stupid drawings. So I crouch beside the drain and slot my artworks into it, one by one, as if through a letterbox. I have no sense of guilt about potentially blocking the system. No thought of what will happen next. Drains are holes in the ground, that's all. Subterranean chambers into which my rubbish can simply disappear. They have always been there and I have no concept of a world before them. I am probably more familiar with drains than I am with rocks or flowers and I have not yet arranged objects into a hierarchy of value. No one thing is necessarily more authentic or less authentic, more natural or less natural, than another. They are all just *things*. New things. Interesting things.

A child's imagination is a creeper vine. It entwines itself around whatever is available, whether it's a lamp post or an oak

3

tree, a pile of rubble or a Saxon barrow. Magnified in the slow time of a child's perception, objects that adults take for granted can seem fantastical. For instance, the canal in Kirkintilloch was a carpet of luminescent green dotted with bottles and cans, so solid in appearance I was certain I could walk on it. Or there was the rugby club in Bishopbriggs where my dad played on Saturday afternoons. As hairy giants thundered through the mud and fought each other to the death, I had freedom to explore the mini grandstand. The door to the storeroom beneath was occasionally unlocked. Inside were sandbags, planks, cones and other random artefacts of rugby club maintenance. Dust danced in the blades of light that sliced between the slats of the wooden seating above me. Strips of white plastic flapped from mysterious earthen mounds. It was like a chamber in the Great Pyramid of Giza and I was an adventurer in an ancient world. Overlooking the rugby club was an 80-foot concrete water tower on long slender legs, a sentient entity that watched me silently from above the treetops, weird and other-worldly. I got a similar thrill from cooling towers, those alien structures on the horizon which gave birth to new clouds. And especially electricity pylons, those metal giants bonded by wire and shackles of glass. I loved to stare out at them on our car journeys from Kirkintilloch into Glasgow, ranged alongside the road from the countryside to the city.

When my family moved from Scotland to Derbyshire, the pylons followed me down the motorway and arranged themselves on the Pennines overlooking my new home town. A few years after the move, I read John Christopher's trilogy of novels about the Tripods, gigantic metal machines operated by aliens, designed to subjugate humans by implanting 'Caps' in their skulls on their fourteenth birthdays. Written in the 1960s, these books were an update of *The War of the Worlds* by H. G. Wells in which the strategy of the invader was more complex than mere brute force, controlling the minds of earthlings through technology instead. By now I was fully aware that pylons hadn't always been here, like the trees and mountains. They were more like the Tripods: ruthless invaders accepted by a subservient populace as an inevitable reality. After all, the pylons brought the electricity that ran my Dad's BBC Micro. They powered the lights. There could be no TV without them. The pylons weren't just striding across the hills, they were inside my home, running things.

Pylons loomed large for the 'haunted generation', a phrase used by broadcaster and writer Bob Fischer to describe those who grew up in the 1970s and early 1980s, influenced by TV programmes such as *Penda's Fen*, *Bagpuss*, *Doctor Who* and *Children of the Stones*. In 1975, there was a children's science fiction series called *The Changes*, based on the novels of Peter Dickinson. It depicted a Britain where electronic devices and machines start to emit a noise so maddening that the populace is driven to smash them to pieces, flee the cities and revert to a superstitious pre-industrial age. In the aftermath, words such as 'tractor' and 'electricity' become so taboo that their utterance can result in a mob beating. The many electricity pylons that remain standing are treated as menacing totems, prompting fear and disgust in Nicky, the teenage protagonist, who calls them 'wicked' and tells her companions that the pylons 'feel like a curse'. Throughout the series, sudden static shots of the pylons fill the screen accompanied by sharp stabs of dark electronica, shooting a jolt of fear through the wide-eyed British viewers sitting transfixed in front of their TVs. Artist and filmmaker Seán Vicary writes:

> I have vivid memories of watching *The Changes* on a huge rented 1970s black-and-white TV, the audio materialising a good few minutes before the picture. Terrifying, I never felt comfortable with the pylon in the nearby field again. The show definitely left its mark as I remember a period of painting black and white pictures of pylons on old cereal boxes.

Alongside these dystopian teatime kids' shows the haunted generation was regaled with public information films depicting all manner of gruesome possibilities: drowning in ponds; being hit by trains; getting bitten by rabid foxes; or being blinded by a firework. In *Play Safe*, a 1978 film about the perils of electrocution, a young boy is flying his kite close to some pylons when it becomes tangled in the overhead power lines, instantly killing him. In another sequence, a boy named Jimmy is urged by his friend to clamber over the fence surrounding a substation to retrieve his Frisbee. As Jimmy touches one of the cables his companion screams and we see Jimmy's legs rigid with shock, flared jeans on fire. The narrator, a cartoon owl with bags under his eyes, warns: 'Electricity can jump gaps and pass through your body to earth.' As the filmmakers no doubt intended, the idea that deadly matter can zap you into oblivion for some slight transgression is the sort of thing that sticks with you as a child. Pylons preyed on joy. They punished carelessness. As the owl reminds us: 'Electricity is a faithful servant but a dangerous master.'

Pylons were good and they were evil. They brought the light of life and the black void of death. They were everyday and they were alien. Their contradictions fascinated me in a way that trees and other natural phenomena never did, which might go a long way to explain my relationship with the electricity pylon on Hackney Marshes.

||||||||||||||||||

In 2007 I got married and bought a flat in Clapton Pond, Hackney, East London. My wife was pregnant, and my days of gallivanting in pubs and clubs were over. It was time to settle down. I bought a cocker spaniel puppy and took him for walks in the nearby park, at the bottom of which was a canalised stretch of the River Lea, known as the Lee Navigation. On the other side of the waterway was the Lea Valley nature reserve, a strip of marshes and woodland in this former industrial heartland, scarred with railway lines and dead aqueducts, reservoirs and derelict factories. It was at around this sa
that I read *The Unofficial Countryside* by acclaimed natu

Richard Mabey. Published in 1973, it describes how nature can flourish in those edges of towns and cities which were never intended for wildlife. These are landscapes not considered to be 'proper' countryside, yet they harbour an array of life and can have as much beauty as the postcard rural Britain of common imagination. Mabey complains that we tend to see nature as something 'over there', like a picture on a wall to be admired, citing the set pieces of the countryside such as forests, meadows and moors where we might head for a weekend's ramble, before we return to our ordinary lives. But, as Mabey points out, the natural world is everywhere. All it takes is a crack in the pavement for a plant to put down roots. There are many urban spaces that provide opportunities for plants and creatures to thrive:

> The water inside abandoned docks and in artificially created reservoirs; canal towpaths, and the dry banks of railway cuttings; allotments, parks, golf courses and gardens; the old trees in churchyards and the scrubby hawthorns at the back end of industrial estates; bomb-sites in old parts of the town and building sites in the new.[1]

As I read *The Unofficial Countryside* I realised I was walking every day through the semi-industrial world that Mabey was describing, where long-horned cattle grazed by the railway lines, herons fished in flooded Blitz bomb craters, and towers of giant hogweed waved their toxic fronds on the river banks. But it wasn't the nature that captivated me so much about this

8

landscape as the many surprising human stories I found flourishing there: the railway arch beneath which the first British aeroplane was built; sightings of phantom bears and crocodiles; tales of Blitz rubble buried beneath the football pitches; doggers in the car park; techno ravers beside the reservoirs. Just like buddleia seeds that settle in a railway siding, the spores of human lore will eventually take root, grow and bloom wherever we dwell for long enough, even in the most hostile places.

What gave the Lea Valley its narrative fertility was its series of eighteenth- and nineteenth-century intrusions: the canals and locks; the railway bridges; the decommissioned Victorian water-filtration plant, abandoned to nature, with trees pushing through the remnants of brickwork and sluice-gate machinery. These industrial structures were rightly revered even by those who campaigned to protect the marshes from the encroachment of roads, leisure facilities and car parks. But I wondered what the difference was between a Victorian railway bridge and a flyover, or between a copper mill and a toilet block, apart from the passage of time. One day, they would all be ruins.

For me, the most striking of the modern invaders were the electricity pylons, which marched in a line up the marshland, along the river, over the reservoirs and out across the industrial estates. One in particular caught my eye. It was the only pylon situated within the ruined reservoir filter beds, towering over the path, its reflection shimmering in a pond. In this Victorian setting the pylon was more like an invention of H. G. Wells than of John Christopher. I loved to stand between its legs and gaze up into the vortex of its reticulated geometry, black against a blue sky, or silver against dark cloud. I'd sit beneath it and listen to its hum, which gradually began to make rhythmical sense as my brain ordered its chaos into patterns and my interior currents began to duet with the power lines. I had strange, impulsive thoughts. The rings of barbed wire around the pylon's struts looked like garters on the legs of a sexy French maid. There was a feminine quality to the pylon's shape, as well as an obviously phallic one. Before long, it became a *she*. I thought she was beautiful, my electricity pylon. And I did think of her as mine, even though I knew it was wrong to feel possessive about a National Grid-owned structure in a public space. Besides, she was many other people's pylon, too. My rival suitors on the marshes began to publish photos of her on Twitter, Instagram, Flickr and Facebook, taken from similar angles. It seemed like everyone wanted a piece of her.

One summer morning, as I approached my pylon, there was a Rastafarian standing on the bench in front of her, facing away, his palms held up to the sky, jigging from leg to leg, singing a reggae-inflected hymn of devotion at the top of his lungs as sunshine glinted on the steel tower behind him. This might not have been coincidental, bearing in mind the origins of the classic British electricity pylon. Designed in the 1920s by architect Sir Reginald Blomfield, the tapered latticed tower with a pyramidion at its apex was inspired by the shape of ancient Egyptian obelisks, which channelled the sun's rays, bringing heat and light from the gods. The etymological origin of the word 'pylon' is a Greek word for 'gateway', more specifically the gateway to an ancient Egyptian temple. These took the form of two towers decorated with reliefs, symbolising the hills on either side of the Nile; the gateway was the sun rising between them, representing creation. The first examples were built in Heliopolis, capital of the Ra sun cult.

In 2010, a Lancashire-based group of 'free thinkers' known as New Horizons published a YouTube video, linking the obelisk design of the British electricity pylon to the shadowy secret society known as the Illuminati. According to the group, the pylons are 'Penis Icons' representative of the sun god Ra, designed by the Illuminati to 'litter the cities and towns of the world – flaunting the hidden Power of the Ruling bloodlines'. Why else, they argue, would such a specific design, which has no practical necessity, have been chosen, if not as a demonstration by the ruling elites of their control? To illustrate their theory, they include clips from a 1991 advert for National Power, which shows sentient pylons crackling into life, tearing their legs free of the earth and striding across the landscape. The ad culminates with pylons standing on the cliffs of England, saluting the sun – or, more specifically, say New Horizons, the sun god Ra.

The first pylon in Britain appeared outside Edinburgh in 1928. By 1933 there were 26,000 of them, which must have been a radical transformation of the skyline. The technological progress in the nascent years of powerlines inspired the work of a group known as the 'Pylon Poets' in the 1930s. The most famous of these poems is 'The Pylons' by Stephen Spender, which contrasts the onslaught of concrete and wire with the rural environment, describing pylons as the 'quick perspective of the future' – the countryside's prophetic dream of the cities yet to come. Pylons were a glimpse of a new Britain, and not always a positive one either. Another member of the group, Stanley Snaith, took a more hostile tack in his poem 'Pylons', suggesting that they would trample down traditions like 'flowers dropped by children', invading our culture with new thoughts and new habits. This fear might seem quaint today, almost a century on. To us, pylons represent an old technology, their structures embedded so deeply in our culture that there are not many people in existence who were born in a world without them. If those 'new habits' described by Stanley Snaith include our reliance on TVs, computers and washing machines, there are very few people who don't have those habits now, and even fewer who live off the grid entirely.

The universality of our dependence on electricity hasn't stopped people from feeling an ongoing resistance to pylons over the past eighty years – especially those who don't wish them to ruin the view. This attitude presupposes that there is a pure, indigenous nature to be contaminated. That the view has not already been altered dramatically by human intervention. But this is far from the case. Ever since hunter gatherers switched to farming the land, storing crops for the future, our relationship with the natural world began to change and fray and the topography became subverted to the human cause. If scientists are correct in postulating a geological age known as the Anthropocene, in which humankind is changing the very fabric of the earth, the process began long before the Jesus Christ of William Blake's imagination walked upon England's green and pleasant land; even before the dark Satanic mills of the industrial revolution. By the seventeenth century the great forests that covered the land had been largely plundered for houses, ships and fuel, while fields had been enclosed for agriculture and ownership by those pretty hedgerows we sentimentalise today. The entirety of the lowland country had been reconfigured for the benefit of humans.

Pylons merely show up that landscape for what it is: shaped by felling, ploughing, seeding and enclosure, grouse rearing and pest control, at the expense of animal and plant diversity. To attack the ugliness of electricity pylons, on which we rely for our daily lives, is to deny the truth of the state we live in, the civilisation we have built and the price we must pay for it. As Richard Mabey pointed out, nature is everywhere. There is no possibility of a trade-off where we can keep nature as a pleasure garden to be admired from afar, so that we can do what we like in towns and cities, where we consume electric power relentlessly. It's all the same world. There is no escape. Taking a pylon down for scenic reasons is like repainting the bow of the *Titanic* as the iceberg looms.

||||||||||||||||||||

In Hackney Marshes, back in 2010, my beloved pylon was under threat too. With the London 2012 Olympics on their way, she was to be removed from her picturesque filter beds. It began with a notification taped to her leg. Then wooden hoardings around her base. Finally, a crane and workers in hats came to pull her apart like a cooked lobster. I was fascinated at the way the power lines from the preceding pylon were disconnected and then angled down into the football pitch, as if delivering energy back into the ancient marshland.

After she was disassembled I wrote a short story called 'A Dream Life of Hackney Marshes',[2] about a new father who falls in love with the pylon. He calls her Angel and makes her playlists of electronic music, spending more and more time with her, until he loses interest in his wife and child entirely. To better connect with his lover, he dabs his eyes with his dog's cataract medicine, flooding his pupils with light so that in his sun-frazzled vision, the pylon assumes the form of Ursula Andress sashaying out of the sea towards James Bond in *Dr No*. When Angel is threatened with removal, he is compelled to defend her in the same way that a tree hugger might defend an historically significant oak, leaping over the hoardings to stay by her side. This is not as strange an idea as it sounds. There is much of the constructed world for which we are perfectly comfortable using impassioned terms of endearment. We can happily admit that we love a house. Love a car. Love a street. Love a city. So why not a pylon?

Besides, I was by no means the only person to have this kind of appreciation. In the years after my story was published, I came across others who used electricity pylons in their work, including Maxim Peter Griffin, a Lincolnshire-based artist who catalogues the contours and colours of the hills, fields and trackways of what he calls 'weird Albion'. Within his elemental topographies he includes modern features such as masts, telegraph poles, wind turbines and pylons. In one of his early works, an angry pylon projects an orange skull-and-crossbones from a hole at its apex, like the Eye of Sauron in Tolkien's trilogy *The Lord of the Rings*. In another, a pylon on the horizon blasts the sun's rays onto a circle of stone megaliths.

Twilight of the Gods by Maxim Griffin.

I also discovered oneirographs (pictures of a dream) by poet and artist James Knight, one of which is entitled *Pylon Christ* and depicts Jesus crucified on the cross-arms of the structure. Then there was Richard Littler's satirical website Scarfolk, which documents a fictional town in north-west England that remains perpetually looped in the 1970s. In a pastiche of a public information poster he depicts an electricity pylon surrounded by children holding ropes, with text announcing the 'Scarfolk May Pylon Dance'. As well as mocking the more blasé approach to health and safety of the 1970s, it suggests that there is something almost cultish about our fascination with these totems of electric power.

There is no reason why the primal instinct to carry out spiritual rites cannot encompass the synthetic as well as the natural, the modern as well as the ancient. There were times on my dog walks in the Lea Valley when I found remnants of campfires and joint butts scattered beneath my pylon, presumably left by fellow devotees who huddled at night beneath her crackling gussets. This is something filmmaker John Rogers also noticed on the marshes, describing it in one of his YouTube videos as 'ritualistic pylon worship'. It is an idea that finds its fullest expression in the work of author David Southwell and his imagined pylon cult. David is the creator of Hookland, an open-source project that depicts a 'lost' English county where our weird old customs are transformed into a fictional collection of folklore, from bizarre murders and apocryphal tales to hauntings and rituals. Hookland isn't a 'merrie olde' rural world but a modern England in which magic and terror can be found in the technologies and culture of the 1960s, 1970s and 1980s.

For instance, his pylon cult, known as the Children of the Hum or the Pylon People, is described by *The Hookland Guide* as a group that began when some youngsters went missing after a free festival in 1969. The legend is that they live a nomadic existence, following the routes of power lines – or 'electric ley lines' – across the country, camping beneath pylons at night to sing their songs of devotion.

Inspired by Southwell's tale, writer and musician Leigh Wright, aka The Ephemeral Man, released what he describes as a 'curio from the Children of the Hum archives'. It is a piece of drone music presented as having been recorded in 1970, in which the clanking of high-tension wires blends with clicks, whoops and wails. Human voices seep into the mix: the songs of children, tinny and warbling, like ghosts in the overhead wires. This eerie soundscape, inspired by Southwell's tales of the lost county of Hookland, would make a fitting soundtrack to a supernatural event that occurred in Yorkshire in 1987.

||||||||||||||||||||

By the mid 1980s the steel town of Stocksbridge was suffering from severe congestion as vehicles left the M1 north of Sheffield to cross the Pennines towards Manchester. To solve this problem, work began in 1987 on the Stocksbridge Bypass. Machines rolled onto the hills and moorland and dug ᵈ the soil, cutting through rock and, some belie spirits of the dead.

17

One night in late September, at around 12.30 a.m., the construction site supervisor received a panicked call from two security guards working the late shift. Steven Brookes and David Goldthorpe had noticed movement by the side of a road called Pea Royd Lane not far from the steelworks and had gone over to investigate. As they entered the muddy field, they saw children dressed in old-fashioned garb skipping and dancing in a circle around an electricity pylon, singing the nursery rhyme 'Ring o' Roses'. But as the security guards drew closer the kids vanished. When they arrived at the spot beneath the pylon there was no sign of them. No footprints in the mud. No tracks. No churned earth to suggest anybody had been there at all. When the guards talked to construction workers staying in caravans overnight near the site, some said that they too had heard children's laughter.

That was the first in a series of hauntings on the bypass, a road that has become notorious for its high death rate. They have included sightings of a headless monk, a black dog and a woman in white, as well as further encounters with the ghostly children, who are reported to have been seen by other drivers playing around the base of the pylons. The website Sheffield Paranormal quotes an anonymous van driver, forced to pull over on the bypass when some gas bottles in the back of his van became loose. He says:

> I saw two little boys in front of my van. They were about eight years old, and I wondered why on earth they were out so late. I thought they must be lost or something. They were both wearing greyish shirts and one had a cap in his

hand, and it was as though he was waving it at me. One lad looked quite happy, and the other didn't look unhappy but he wasn't smiling like the other one. I couldn't see below their waists because I was in a transit van and the dashboard stopped any more of a view. Then when I got out to look they had gone.[3]

The Stocksbridge bypass takes traffic to the Woodhead Pass, which winds over the Pennines to Glossop in Derbyshire, the town where I grew up in the 1980s. Although I must have travelled on this road at least once or twice as a child, perhaps on the way to visit my parents' friends in Sheffield or to reach the M1, I could not remember it. But when I learned about the Stocksbridge haunting I decided I'd take a drive along the bypass to hunt for the pylon children, then cross the Pennines in search of the pylons of my own youth, to see how they looked to me now.

I left the M1 near Junction 35 and took the A616 towards the bypass. As soon as I approached the haunted road, an uncannily heavy fog descended. The roadside lamps glowered yellow, even though it was only four o'clock on a June afternoon. This theatrical scene felt put on for my benefit, the opaque terrain now pregnant with supernatural possibilities. I could just about see the pylons poking out over the tops of the trees as the road cut through the lush green peaks, crisscrossed with telegraph wires, concrete footbridges flipping past overhead. Eventually I passed signs for 'steelworks access', and my eyes yearned for the pylon ghost children to emerge from the fog. Even as I looked, I was aware that if I did spot a ghost beneath the pylons of Britain's most haunted bypass, nobody would believe that I wasn't making it up for this book. But I also knew that if I were to see something it would be at a time like this, for when twilight falls and fog shrouds the familiar, we are most likely to glimpse apparitions from the otherworld.

What was most uncanny was the way the fog dissipated the instant I left this stretch of road and turned onto the Woodhead Pass, precipitating into a fine drizzle. I drove a twisted route towards the town in which I grew up, sweeping alongside a reservoir through a Jurassic Park of pylons, with an amazing variety of shapes – some tall and treelike, fat mega pylons with legs splayed between two sides of the valley, and smaller ones with arms slinging power lines in three directions, their geometry glistering in the rain. They were like Sherpas guiding me through the mountains towards my former home. I could sense how they might have impressed me as a child, the way they ranged the valley on slopes of fern and bracken or stood by the water in a teeth-clenching mix of electricity and liquid, life and death.

This is why so many people are drawn to pylons. They bring excitement to the topography and give it a narrative. In *Scarp*, the autobiographical novel by Nick Papadimitriou about a man obsessed with a ridge of land along the Middlesex–Hertfordshire border, the protagonist arrives at a place where 'a particularly strident line of pylons follows the stream's course and adds a peculiar intensity to the landscape'. It strikes him as 'a place of history and power, one of those Celtic "thin places", where a sense of something other lurks just behind the visible'. Rather than detracting from the landscape the pylons intensify Papadimitriou's sense of the landscape's folkloric essence. I can remember having the same feeling when I took a walk through the ancient Brede High Woods in East Sussex. Along the trail I passed several memorial benches, positioned in leafy enclaves, or on picturesque vantage points, bearing dedications from loved ones. There is nothing unusual in this. The proliferation of such benches in public places is symptomatic of what writer and social historian Ken Worpole describes as a return to 'older practices of informal memorialisation'.[4] Benches are usually located where someone used to sit and look out over a landscape, or where they enjoyed significant moments. The idea is that the passer-by who sits on this bench and gazes outwards invigorates the memory of the dead person who might have done the same. What was unusual in Brede High Woods was that I found a memorial bench looking directly out over a corridor of electricity pylons that certainly predated the bench, suggesting that it was there because the deceased appreciated this view, that the pylons meant something to them, or were somehow intrinsic to an important moment in their life.

Perhaps a similar emotional connection inspired the eerie case of the Pylon Man of Wigan. One cold winter morning in 2013, a man was walking his dog across wasteland near Westwood Power Station just outside Wigan, when he noticed something odd. A lone figure appeared to be standing perfectly still beneath one of the electricity pylons, silhouetted against the sky. As the walker drew closer, he realised that it was a man hanging by his neck from one of the struts. When the police arrived, all they found in the dead man's pockets was £85, some tobacco and a bus ticket to Wigan. During the investigation, they were unable to identify the deceased through his fingerprints or DNA. His olive complexion suggested that he might be from the Middle East, but despite pleas for information in the media, nobody ever came forward. The Pylon Man has become a local mystery. Who was he? Why would he travel all the way to that particular spot and choose that structure to end his life? Perhaps he simply made a snap decision when he saw the pylon. Or perhaps it reminded him of something in his past, for better or worse.

Pylons can become anchor points for significant memories, helping us to summon up a particular time and place. Poet Annie Muir captures this beautifully in the final lines of a poem inspired by a pylon near Sale Water Park in Greater Manchester:

> she is the shed skin of a moment in your life. A monument
> to the here and now
>
> like a photo of you with a different haircut
> or a pair of old shoes
>
> tied to your new ones by the laces
> but trailing behind, covered in mud.[5]

Pylons certainly present me with an old picture of my younger self, thinking back to when I was that naive little boy, who thought that there were caves beneath drains, that he could walk on green canals, and that the metal towers that delivered electricity into his home were terrifying Tripods, hell-bent on mind control. These extraordinary structures remain objects of fascination, awe and fear for me today – though for different reasons. In my innocent childhood days, energy seemed limitless and our technological progress without serious consequence. This has been superseded by anxiety about the irreversible harm our plundering of the earth's resources has done to the climate, wildlife and our water support systems. What price we must now pay for our dependency on fossil fuels we will find out in the near future as the planet rapidly warms. But pylons are merely messengers of this truth, not the cause. They are equally capable of delivering energy produced by solar and wind farms. Unlike *The Changes*, in which people turn against them with anger, we might find salvation in these towers, embracing their necessity instead of living in denial.

|||||||||||||||||

Against the clear blue sky
In Sun Ra's bright abode
The pylon host on high
Brings energy from the gods
Alleluia
The children sing
Dance in a ring
Alleluia

But the gods deliver fear
Through the hum of pylon song
A torment for all to hear
The sun shone all along
Alleluia
The stranger hung
From the bottom rung
Alleluia

O erotic angel, truth
To all thy lovers impart
And teach us in our youth
To know and fear your art
Alleluia
The ghosts shall sing
In the Reckoning
Alleluia

2

ENERGY CIRCLES

THE POWER OF
RING ROADS AND
ROUNDABOUTS

I n 1306, Robert the Bruce, King of the Scots, was in trouble. He had been defeated by the English, his wife captured, and three of his brothers executed. Now he was hiding in a cave on an island off the north coast of Ireland. The legend goes that at this lowest point in his life he derived inspiration from a spider trying to spin its web on a wall. The spider kept falling and clambering back up its thread to persevere with its feat of engineering. Robert realised that, like the spider, he too must persist in his aim to liberate Scotland, despite disastrous recent setbacks and the overwhelming task ahead. Eight years later, he led his nation to independence after victory at Bannockburn.

Flash forward to Scotland in the middle of the twentieth century, and another Robert Bruce had his own geometric challenge to face. An engineer for Glasgow Corporation, he had written a radical report suggesting that the city's historical centre be demolished to create a clean slate for redevelopment. By the end of the Second World War, much of the city's Victorian housing was dilapidated, with families squeezed into overcrowded slums and many streets all but destroyed by Blitz bombing. Disease and discontent were rife. A fresh solution was required, and Bruce believed he had the answer. Instead of removing people from the city centre, sending them to satellite towns and overspill suburbs, they would be rehomed within socially engineered housing schemes. The Bruce Report, published in 1945, proposed a futuristic layout of long, wide avenues and green spaces, with the city centre divided into zones of usage. A system of motorways would form a giant orbital box around the city with interchanges on each corner to feed traffic in and out.

As he agonised over the future of Scotland's biggest city, dreaming of its liberation from disease and social decay, did Robert Bruce, like his kingly namesake, draw inspiration from the orbital structure of a spider's web? Did he take heed of the powerful concentric threads of its construction and how the spider linked them together to create a system in which it would thrive? Perhaps it's a fanciful thought but it's hard not to see something web-like in Bruce's proposed design. A ring road with interconnecting routes would allow the city to become highly organised along fresh lines, entirely disconnected from the historical Glasgow, over which would be laid a brand new pattern. It was an extreme solution which met with fierce opposition but it was nonetheless approved by the Glasgow Corporation in 1947. It seemed as if Bruce was about to achieve the impossible: the complete demolition, then rebirth, of a city. It was his Bannockburn, his chance to go down in legend not only for recreating Glasgow, but for laying down the template for all future British cities.

Alas for Bruce, two years later the project was cancelled on grounds of cost, but it wasn't quite the end of his orbital dream. In the 1960s, work began on the north and west sides of what was to be an inner ring road, based on the motorway 'box' recommended by the Bruce Plan. For over a decade, wrecking balls smashed through the buildings of Anderston, Garnethill, Townhead, Charing Cross and Cowcaddens to angry protests from the communities who lived there. Historically significant buildings were torn down. Entire streets vanished from the map. And then this project, too, was abandoned in the 1970s, leaving behind a half-built inner ring road that, to this day, exerts a cultish influence on Glasgow, like a dream of the 'One Ring' which the Gollum-like city cannot shake. A glimpse of an alternative, almost mythical, structure for the city, the geometry of which can only now be deduced, never seen in full.

The most enduring legacy of the inner ring road is the M8 motorway, which cuts across the north of the city centre, jammed with vehicles, skirting close to the Necropolis – the city's famous Victorian cemetery – and then past Glasgow Cathedral and the Royal Infirmary, at which point a tangle of flyovers and access ramps whirls the traffic off the motorway and south into the historical city, or north towards Springburn. When I decided to explore this corner of Glasgow on foot, I was not particularly interested in the ring road. I was simply out on a walk, looking for stories. After all, there are plenty of actually completed ring roads in Britain, so why would a half-built one be of interest? This is precisely what made my curious discovery that day even more of a surprise.

||||||||||||||||||

After descending the steep hill of the Necropolis, I cut through the grounds of the Cathedral. Almost as soon as the gothic architecture fell away behind me, I beheld the great beast of the motorway interchange, a concrete Cthulhu flinging out its access-road tentacles. Had Bruce's plan come to fruition there would have been four interchanges like this on each corner of the inner ring road, clutching central Glasgow in their mighty grip. Beneath the M8 flyover I entered a hotchpotch underworld of cobbled slopes, pathways, stone plinths and steps. On a raised platform was a series of brick walls, about shoulder height, which look like speculative rooms in a half-built house. It could have been a ruin or an aborted idea, like Bruce's alternative Glasgow. I followed a raised verge alongside the dual carriageway then under the A803. That's when I caught sight of something taped to a pillar rising from the paved bank on the other side of the railing: two sheets of paper flapping in the backdraft of a passing truck, both containing maps. It didn't make sense: why would there be maps stuck to a pillar where neither drivers nor pedestrians could see them?

I vaulted the railings and slid on my backside down the bank, careful not to tumble into the traffic. Glued to the pillar was a printout of 'The City of Glasgow Planning Report, Folio No. 6: THE INNER CORE OF THE CITY'– an image from the Bruce Report. Next to it, a map of Glasgow, over which the complete motorway ring road was drawn in black ink, a curl of flyover interchanges on each corner. I felt conspicuous on the weed-strewn slabs, hand on the pillar to steady myself, as I

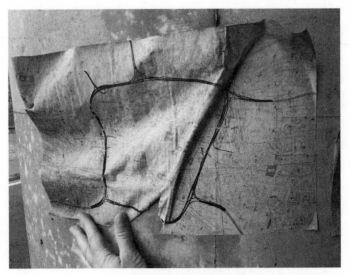

A map of Bruce's inner ring road,
found beneath a flyover.

tried to understand what I was looking at and why it was here.
It was hard to know if I was staring at a remnant of a geog-
raphy project, an artistic intervention, the work of a ring-road
obsessive propagating Bruce's ideas seventy-five years later, or
a protest against the destruction his vision had caused to local
communities. It was a weird object, seemingly intended for the
attention of nobody, placed in an obscure location without easy
access, and yet here I was, looking at it.

There is an esoteric practice known as urban geomancy, in
which apparently accidental signs, symbols and juxtapositions
can be 'read', much like Tarot cards, tea leaves or runes, allowing us to divine messages from the cosmos – the interpretation

of the finder being more important than any objective answer. Usually, these messages take the form of letters, shapes and symbols found on roads and walls, in discarded rubbish, graffiti and eroded posters but it's rarely something as specific and pro-saic as an actual map. What could my mysterious map mean? After all, here was a depiction of an imaginary Glasgow that never quite came to be, stuck onto a pillar beneath a flyover on an aborted motorway ring road.

What struck me most, looking at the map, was the box drawn over the city, tracing a speculative city above the real one. The idea that there are hidden layers to Glasgow – both real and imagined – is a recurring theme in the city, which has been the subject of two attempts to uncover a secret geometry beneath its modern layout.* The first was by Ludovic McLellan Mann (1869–1955), an insurance broker who moonlighted as an amateur archaeologist. In the early 1900s he carried out excava-tions of Neolithic sites across Scotland, publishing papers and organising exhibitions. By 1915 he had become fascinated by cup-marks – circular depressions etched in stone by prehistoric peoples. Examining one such example – the Langside Stone – in a museum, he theorised that the rings were early records of eclipses: 'The cupped stones are registers made by prehis-toric astronomers who reckoned time by hours, days, years,

---

* For more on this topic, I highly recommend Kenneth Brophy's essay on Ludovic McLellan Mann and Harry Bell, 'Glasgow's occult ancient geometry' in *Folk Horror Revival: Urban Wyrd* (Wyrd Harvest Press, 2019).

and long cycles of years. The happening of eclipses punctuated their cycles.'

This was the beginning of an obsession about links between the terrestrial and the celestial. By the 1930s, he was convinced that the arrangement of key topographical locations across Glasgow was evidence of prehistoric moon worship. 'Glasgow is rich in places named after the Moon divinity,' he wrote. 'The Moon God, Clot, gave his name to the river, the Clota or Clyde, because the stream at Glasgow made a magnificent sweep in its course, imitative of the new moon.' Not only did he believe that many place names bore traces of lunar lore, but that the arrangement of ancient sites had a pattern:

> The Neolithic philosopher and astronomer laid out the Glasgow area on a plan similar to that of a clock-face and like a gigantic spider's web, but rigorously geometrical. Its radii, usually set on a nineteenth divisional system (sub-divided at times into 38ths and 76ths), dictated the positions, and ran through loci, of prehistoric importance. These lines were counted anti-clockwise, beginning at the south-going radius which corresponds with the position of the clock-hand which indicates six o'clock on a modern timepiece.[6]

Mann's perception of an orbital design hidden beneath Glasgow has echoes in both Robert Bruce's ring-road vision and the spider web that inspired Robert the Bruce. The story of the Scottish king and the persistent arachnid is apocryphal, made up by Sir Walter Scott in 1828, and perhaps Mann's vision of a sacred geometry beneath the modern streets is also a work of fiction – selectively picking out the features that align with his model. Nonetheless he correctly portrayed a prehistoric world that was more philosophically complex and astronomically sophisticated than many academics of the time believed. His ambitious ideas attempted to connect the modern Glasgow with an ancient people who had endowed the city with its place names, showing that the old myths are not all dead and can still resonate for those who care to look.

In the 1980s, a second amateur archaeologist, Harry Bell, was influenced by the ideas of Mann as well as those of Alfred Watkins, whose book *The Old Straight Track* (1925) describes hidden lines in the English countryside that link important locations such as standing stones, castles, churches and cairns. He called them 'prehistoric communication lines' but later named them 'ley lines'. Up in Scotland, almost sixty years later, Bell drew a series of them radiating out from Glasgow to various ancient castles, settlements, rock art sites and crags in the surrounding countryside. Critics often sneer about ley lines and their hunters, dismissing the idea as pseudoscientific bunkum, but Mann, Bell and Watkins were not necessarily trying to tap into mystic energy channels. Rather, they were looking for evidence of prehistoric cultures in the landscape, from a time before maps and writing, the stories of which they might be able to ascertain, with a little imagination, by studying the land. They used points of topographical interest to trace what might have been popular routes for traders, pilgrims and priests, who travelled beaten tracks between important places, much as ring roads, link roads and motorways form welts in the landscape today, joining towns across the countryside and spinning geometric webs around our cities. Twelve of Bell's lines interconnected at the city's Necropolis, either stopping at it or running through it. He believed that this low but prominent hill had been a locus of power since prehistory, and it is – perhaps not coincidentally – very close to where I found the mysteriously placed map of the Bruce Plan, near the M8 interchange where so many roads converge like ley lines, connecting the city to other places of significance.

Bell published his findings in a pamphlet called *Glasgow's Secret Geometry: The City's Oldest Mystery*. This later inspired the Glaswegian filmmaker May Miles Thomas, who discovered that one of Bell's sacred lines ran through her childhood home and primary school. At the same time, she stumbled on the story of Mary Ross, who in 1959 suffered mental health problems after she gave birth out of wedlock to a child, who was taken away for adoption. Ross was committed as a psychiatric patient in Glasgow's Leverndale Hospital, then known as the Hawkshead Asylum. After thirty years she was released under the Care in the Community Act, whereupon she embarked on a series of drifting journeys through Glasgow in search of the daughter she had lost.

Miles Thomas realised that Mary's journeys overlapped with many of the places that Bell visited while conducting research for *Glasgow's Secret Geometry*. Her resulting film, *The Devil's Plantation*, a series of static landscape shots with a spoken narrative, links the stories of Bell and Ross, imagining them wandering the city, unknowingly tracing the same ancient geometry in their search for the past, completely unaware of each other despite perhaps even crossing paths as they walked.* In one scene, Mary Ross visits her childhood neighbourhood, partially demolished to make way for Bruce's ring road. In a magnificent shot the M8 in the distance is framed by two Victorian buildings in the foreground: the Grey Dunn biscuit factory and St Margaret Mary's School. The legacy of Bruce's futuristic dream cuts across the skyline of the old city that it had originally sought to destroy. In making the film, May Miles Thomas has added yet another layer to a story that began with the moon cults of the pre-Neolithic and that might yet lure more wanderers down its lines of landscape, even after civilisation crumbles and Glasgow is but a series of mounds in a forest, to be traced by dreamers of the future, keen to learn what we believed and why we were no more.

While Mann and Bell read pagan ideas into topographical features and place names, there are those who see those same resonances in modern orbital structures. Stuart Silver is a Glasgow-based 'urban druid' who, along with Andy Hokano,

---

* May Miles Thomas adds: 'Ross's timeline of events wasn't the most reliable but certainly she absconded from Leverndale on numerous occasions so it's possible she visited the same sites as Bell prior to the publication of *Glasgow's Secret Geometry* in 1984.'

formed the Psychogeographical Commission in 2008 to explore the built environment using magical practices, city walks, experimental music and field recordings. Their 2011 piece *Widdershins* explores the occult potential of the Glasgow subway system, the inner circle on which underground trains travel anti-clockwise – or, as the Scots say, 'widdershins'. In folklore, to travel widdershins was considered unlucky, or unholy, for it was to go counter to the movement of the sun and therefore against the flow of nature. Conversely a clockwise direction brought good fortune and harmony with the cosmos: in Celtic culture, funeral processions would circle a burial site clockwise before the body came to rest; when giving a blessing it was customary to walk around the recipient thrice clockwise; and if a ship needed to turn, it always did so clockwise to avoid bad luck.

On the day the Glasgow subway opened in 1896, the unlucky widdershins direction of its inner line wreaked its inevitable misfortune when there was a collision beneath the River Clyde, injuring four people. The accident coated the train wheels in blood, which was smeared around the circuit – a grim echo of human sacrifice. To this day Silver and Hokano consider the widdershins circling of the city's underground train to be a 'constant banishing ritual performed daily upon the whole of the west side of Glasgow' and they have sought to undo it by carrying out their own ritual. On the winter solstice eclipse in 2010, the duo made an audio recording as they travelled clockwise around the outer circle of the subway, beginning and ending at Hillhead Station. Then, in February 2011, they played it back while travelling widdershins on the inner line. They also turned the recording, with its orchestra of squealing train wheels, sliding doors, hissing brakes and hollering wind, into a twenty-six-minute drone piece, which the band released later that year. Asked why he chooses to pursue druidic practices in such a starkly contemporary setting, Silver said: 'I've been a pagan for many years but I also live in a city. It always struck me as a bit odd that most pagans are only really pagans on weekends when they go somewhere green.'[7]

Paganism and the rituals of its practice developed in a rural era, which makes it difficult to pursue in urban areas where rivers are culverted, grass has given way to concrete and light pollution blocks out the stars. But for Silver, that doesn't mean paganism cannot adapt to urban structures, or that magic cannot be performed amid tower blocks, motorways, pavements and subways. He believes that if people re-harmonise with the environment in which they live their daily lives, they can find spiritual and psychological benefits. For instance, pagans believe the circle to be a sacred space, much like a church except that it can be created anywhere, consecrating any ground temporarily and, equally, any existing circle can become magical. For the Psychogeographical Commission, Glasgow's subway transit system was one such circle. But this could also apply to orbital roads, which form even larger rings around our cities. These are maligned as inhospitable, uninspiring and polluted necessities of transport infrastructure but, for one man, a ring road offered sanctuary from his demons and turned him into a holy figure.

Born in Poland in 1920, Józef Stawinoga joined the German army after Hitler invaded his country in the early stages of the Second World War. Sent to Africa to fight under Field Marshal Rommel, he was captured and imprisoned by the Allies in Egypt and endured years of hard labour. When he was liberated, Stawinoga emigrated to Britain, where he secured a job at the steelworks in Bilston, two miles south-east of Wolverhampton, and, in 1952, married an Austrian woman named Hermine Weiss. She left him a year later, which some believe caused a nervous breakdown that precipitated his withdrawal from society. He took to wandering the streets of Wolverhampton in an increasingly bedraggled state, sporting a long beard and pushing his possessions in a pram. In the 1970s he set up a tent on the central reservation of the A4150 inner ring road where he remained a virtual hermit until his death in 2007. The council let him stay there and, in return, he would sweep up leaves. The author Rowena Macdonald, who grew up in the town in the 1980s, recalls him being a familiar sight. 'He looked like a Biblical character. Someone out of time, or timeless. Really, he was more like a mendicant.'*

<hr />

* 'The tramp was one of several local eccentrics,' says Rowena, 'including the man dressed as a cowboy who would stride through the town centre declaring to all that he was the "true cowboy of Wolverhampton"; or Ezra, the Jamaican Evangelical preacher who'd tell people, "Say a prayer before you get to Tettenhall."'

Stawinoga enjoyed regular gifts of clothes, blankets and freshly cooked delicacies from local Hindus who saw him as a holy man. Dershan Lalshadha, Chairman of Wolverhampton's Krishna Mandir Temple, told the BBC: 'In India we believe that people who live in jungles and outskirts, away from civilisation, devote their lives to God. This man doesn't want any relation with the world, he is connected with God and so we believe he is a saintly person.'[8] It is significant, I think, that Wolverhampton's Hindus saw the central reservation as being 'away' from civilisation, even when it was an intrinsic part of the urban infrastructure. Somehow, Stawinoga had turned this section of the ring road into a parallel world in which he could step outside time, and exist beyond the norms of society, without money, a mortgage, or a job, letting devout locals bring him everything he needed for four decades, while shaking his broom cantankerously at anyone who bothered him. It was an act of remarkable wizardry.

In Stuart Silver's druidic view of the city, a ring road has powerful pagan potential, being a gyratory system that facilitates the flow of energy, distributing traffic to important destinations, much in the way that ley lines were routes leading to influential locations. As the moon orbits the earth, and the earth orbits the sun, so we orbit our towns and cities, using roundabouts to propel ourselves in new directions, much like space probes use the gravity of planets to slingshot themselves across the solar system. A roundabout is designed to avoid the stop–start disruptions of a junction and maintain a flow of traffic, with the smoothest possible transition from one road to another. Silver speculates about an alternative Britain in which councils would commonly employ a druid to decide where best to position roundabouts for the most harmonious flow of energy. The druid would look like you or me, he insists, no robes and wooden staffs, just a bloke in a hard hat and suit. 'It would make as much sense as most local council planning decisions anyway,' he says. This reminds me of the tale that the locations of Telford's roundabouts were based on coffee-cup stains left on a map of the proposed construction by twenty council town planners during a meeting. Not realising that the marks were accidental, the contractors simply positioned the roundabouts on the location of the stains. Perhaps this is just a myth, but I like to think that those coffee-cup runes, cast accidentally by unwitting planners, somehow tapped into occult energy lines, which would make Telford's the UK's first esoteric roundabout system.

More overtly pagan are those roundabouts which contain standing stones, like the Coul Roundabout in the Fife town of Glenrothes, which contains a faux-Neolithic circle made from seven tall, flat blocks. It made quite an impression on me when I visited it one summer. Approaching it on foot via an avenue of towering conifers known as Huntsman's Road, it felt appropriate that the stone-circle roundabout would stand at the end of this impressive causeway and at the intersection of four important routes. As I prepared to cross over the road to reach the centre of the roundabout, I felt a tingle of transgression when the driver of a passing car stared suspiciously at me, but once I was within the stone circle, a calm descended, as if I was in the eye of a hurricane. I felt protected, much like Józef Stawinoga might have done on the central reservation of the Wolverhampton ring road.

The Coul Roundabout is a facsimile of a Neolithic ceremonial site only five minutes' walk away. Balfarg Henge once consisted of a series of timber circles and two stone circles, with a burial chamber in the centre. Today there remain only a few stones and replica stumps where the wooden posts would once have stood, set inside a disc of lawn, ringed by a road of houses, almost like a roundabout. I took a cursory look at the information board and strolled across the green, feeling uncomfortably conscious that I was in full view of the houses. I didn't enjoy my experience of the henge as much as I did its recreation on the Coul Roundabout. After all, Balfarg Henge was nothing more than a few scattered remnants of a community long lost, along with its beliefs, culture and language. But on Coul Roundabout the standing stones were visible to a constant flow of motorists, vibrating with the energy of passing machines. Despite its fabricated nature, it was a functioning entity, standing at the intersection of routes, dispersing travellers to places of importance. Experientially, the henge at Coul Roundabout was far superior. It was *alive*.

Kenneth Brophy, a senior lecturer in Archaeology and Prehistory at the University of Glasgow, is known as the Urban Prehistorian. He writes on his blog that 'there is no better indication of the crashing together of prehistory and our modern urban world than roads and cars competing for the same spaces as standing stones'. As a literal example of this he points to an incident in 2011, in which a BMW reversed into the six-foot-tall Bedd Morris bluestone in Pembrokeshire, Wales, and toppled it over, revealing Neolithic hammers and stone flakes, which would not have otherwise been found. 'All our encounters with traces of the past – material and otherwise – happen in the contemporary, the modern,' he writes. 'The past and present meet at a stark and jagged edge, a tear, that for a moment gives the illusion of a past that still exists in a degraded form.'[9] Roundabouts in particular, says Brophy, are a legitimate fieldwork target. He gives the example of the Greenyards Roundabout near Bannockburn in Stirling, the construction of which in 2010 exposed post holes, Bronze Age roundhouses and evidence of agricultural activity. Sites like this offer an opportunity to peer through portals into the past. But it's not only about looking back. Brophy believes that the roundabout has its own inherent value as 'the latest aspect of the biography of this location'.

It was the Urban Prehistorian website that first alerted me to the fact that some roundabouts are listed in the National Monuments Record of Scotland (NMRS)* along with stone circles, architecturally important buildings and public sculptures.

---

* The National Monument Record of Scotland (NMRS) recently changed its name to the National Record of the Historic Environment, but it is still interesting, and very telling, that recent roundabouts are included in such a thing.

These include the Torrance Roundabout in East Kilbride and the Muirhead Roundabout in Cumbernauld. They are surprising choices, because they don't have the kind of distinguishing features you might see on the Coul Roundabout in Glenrothes. As Brophy writes: 'In a town that is, in a sense, defined by its roundabouts the Torrance Roundabout is not even the most interesting roundabout in East Kilbride.' However, many other roundabouts are adorned with artworks and artefacts designed not only to catch the eye but to tell a story about the place in which they are located.

In Morecambe's Central Retail Park, for instance, the roundabouts are populated by sculptures of seabirds, celebrating its coastal heritage. In Birmingham, a roundabout contains sculptures of Spitfires, created by Tim Tolkien, the great-nephew of J. R. R. Tolkien, to commemorate the Castle Bromwich factory where the planes were manufactured. In Ironbridge, a roundabout contains a mine-wheel while the Cuilfail Tunnel Roundabout in Lewes, East Sussex, boasts a sculpture of an ammonite fossil, commonly found in the nearby chalk cliffs. We have come to confer significance on roundabouts like these, transforming them into capsules of local cultural identity.* In some cases, they preserve the past, like the Charles Cross Roundabout in Plymouth which contains a ruined church. The original building was commissioned by King Charles I, but not completed until 1658, by which time the king was dead. It

---

* With thanks to Stuart Silver for the phrase 'capsules of local cultural identity'.

was destroyed during a night of German bombing in 1941 but partially restored to maintain the structure's integrity, before becoming encircled by a gyratory and preserved as a memorial to those Plymouth civilians who died in the Blitz.

Most mysterious in their cultural purpose are the roundabouts of the vast Cribbs Causeway Retail Park near the M5, which I visited in 2014 to carry out research for my book *Car Park Life*. Opposite the entrance to the rear car park of the complex I found a mini-roundabout containing a standing stone that I assumed represented the Neolithic farming origins of commerce that eventually led to capitalist mega-structures such as the retail park. Then came a second roundabout containing a large cone of grass, topped with what looked like a metallic nipple, which I interpreted as a futuristic counterpart to the more traditional standing stone. However, after I posted an article on Unofficial Britain about my research trip, this comment appeared from a reader:

> There are more wondrous roundabouts at Cribbs Causeway – and when you have seen them all you suddenly realise that the designers have had one over on the planners ... They are all erogenous zones. The monolith is an erect winky, the pyramid is a booby complete with nipple, there is a tree sprouting out of a dainty ring-piece and the fourth is a lovely vulva reminiscent of a taco. It's incredible.

Winky? Ring-piece? Booby? Vulva? On a second visit, my attention properly tuned to the roundabouts, I went from the menhir erection to one which did look remarkably like a vulva: two semi-circular mounds with a gash of vegetation between. In the centre of the complex was the breast of the nipple-topped grass cone roundabout and, yes, there was also a roundabout with a tree in its central ring. Perhaps it's true that the planners had something on their mind beyond retail architecture. Perhaps these roundabouts were a subliminal attempt to arouse shoppers so that they shopped with hot-blooded abandon, or they were the work of a secret sex cult operating for reasons as yet unknown, but which one day might become heinously apparent.

IIIIIIIIIIIIIIIIII

Although the first British roundabout appeared in Letchworth Garden City in 1909, they are largely a phenomenon of the late twentieth century, proliferating after 1966 when a new law dictated that approaching traffic must give way to vehicles already on the gyratory. Before that, crossroads were the norm for allowing cars, horses, carts and pilgrims to converge and switch directions, north, south, east or west. Crossroads have a huge significance in global folklore, in which they commonly represent a threshold between worlds, where spirits can manifest. In Romania, they're a meeting point for vampires and witches. Danish lore says that to contact loved ones in the underworld, you must stand at a crossroads and call out the name of the ghost with whom you wish to speak. In African American mythology, the devil appears at the crossroads to bestow on a traveller a talent in return for their soul – a story once used by some to account for the virtuoso ability of Mississippi-born blues guitarist Robert Johnson. In the Isle of Man, children were told that to banish bad fortune they should go where four roads meet and sweep the crossroads until it was clean.

Many crossroads in Britain were turned into roundabouts to allow for better traffic flow, a circle shape overlaid on the cross,* but did they also inherit their lore? There are some suggestions that they did. For instance, the Black Cat Roundabout near the hamlet of Chawston in Bedfordshire used to be a crossroads junction. It got its name from the Black Cat Garage, a car repair shop in the 1920s that used a black cat sign to attract motorists. So iconic did the sign become that in 2004, after the new roundabout was installed, the residents of Chawston arranged for a steel black cat to be placed at its centre. Black cats are traditionally associated with witchcraft, being familiars for practitioners of the dark arts, able to change into human form to spy for their masters. They represent both good and bad fortune, depending on where in the world you are. The Black Cat Roundabout has inherited some of the animal's shape-shifting mystique. The first cat was removed when the roundabout was enlarged, then replaced with a bigger version. That second cat was then stolen in 2007 by persons unknown, leaving locals bereft of their cherished landmark. The following year a third

* This is also the design of the Celtic cross, which is said to have been a marriage of the Christian cross with the pagan circle used to represent the sun god or the moon goddess.

– even larger – black cat was erected only for the stolen second cat to simultaneously and mysteriously reappear on another roundabout at Caldecote, fifteen miles to the south. This second cat was then reinstalled but disappeared again, ending up in Sunderland,* while the third black cat was damaged in 2013 and had to be replaced once more.

Such incidents of skulduggery and misfortune are ongoing, most recently in 2019, when the latest version of the cat was graffitied with white paint, giving it a sinister toothy grin and crazed eyes. The Black Cat Roundabout has become a zone of chaos, uncertainty and nocturnal hijinks, with myriad vanishings and reappearances of its animal familiar – behaviour worthy of a classic folkloric crossroads. And all in less than twenty years. Imagine the stories that might gather around it over the course of centuries to come.

It is not the only unusual case where a roundabout has inherited the lore of the crossroads it replaced. The White Tree Roundabout is just north of Bristol city centre, located on the Downs, an area of parkland bordering Clifton and Redland. It is a confluence of four roads from north, south, east and west, intersecting the A4018 with Parry's Lane. A tree with the lower half of its trunk painted white has stood at this location for at least 150 years and nobody knows why. Back in the nineteenth century, it would likely have been a forbidding, remote

---

* Perhaps not uncoincidentally, 'Black Cats' is the nickname of the Sunderland football team.

place where thieves lurked and men came to solicit sex, so some believe that the tree was originally painted white to tell coachmen to turn off at the junction for a coaching inn, where travellers could stay safe overnight. Another story maintains that the tree was painted by a man who would get drunk in the pubs of Clifton and then struggle to find his way back home in the dark without the white trunk as a marker. And yet another theory is that George Ames, a resident of a nearby mansion named Cote House, painted the tree in the 1840s as a waymark to guide his children's tutor off the Downs. Whether true or not, this last version of the story has led subsequent owners of Cote House to have their gardener reapply the paint every few years.

When the roundabout was installed at the crossroads in 1951, the original tree (if indeed there were no earlier ones) was removed and replaced by an elm tree a few metres from the original spot, and this took on the white paint mantle until it became diseased and was felled in the 1970s. Again, the tradition was not allowed to die. Residents of a local old people's home organised a petition to replace it with the lime tree which stands there today, and its coat of white paint is refreshed every few years as part of the duties of the Downs rangers, possibly much to the relief of phantom coach-drivers and ghost drunkards who use its nocturnal glow to navigate their way through a horde of spectral prostitutes and phantasmic Johns. The species of tree has changed, its position moved and the junction at which it stands transformed into a roundabout, but the legend of the white tree lives on. No one really knows how the custom started, but its continuation matters because it links the past to the present. Another example of how local lore can be sustained by the rings of power that connect the ley lines of our contemporary road network.

||||||||||||||||||

O gin I were whaur the ring road rins,
Whaur the ring road rins, whaur the ring road rins,
O gin I were whaur the ring road rins
At the back o' this city

Aince mair to hear the ancients sang,
To wander roundabouts amang
Wi' friends and fav'rites left sae lang
In the depths o' history

O gin I were whaur the ring road rins,
Whaur the ring road rins, whaur the ring road rins,
O gin I were whaur the ring road rins
Round the back o' this city

How mony a day in Summertime
By the standin' stones still in my prime
Saunterin' the magic circle of time
Wonderin' at its mystery

O gin I were whaur the ring road rins,
Whaur the ring road rins, whaur the ring road rins,
O gin I were whaur the ring road rins
Round the back o' this city

3

DEMONS IN THE PRESENT

THE HAUNTING OF HOUSING ESTATES

One icy evening in mid December, I checked into Grimsby's recently re-opened Yarborough Hotel, a grand four-storey Victorian building in front of the railway station. Extensively renovated after a twenty-year period as a pub, this Wetherspoons-owned hotel is reputedly haunted; before the refurbishment works were carried out, ghost hunters had reported eerie noises and unexplained movements in its shadowy nooks, including a phantom in a white shirt and glasses on its impressive staircase. I saw nothing unusual as I made my way to the first floor, except for the carpet in the corridor: a dark-blue weave, striated with horizontal lines, interrupted by swirls of white and brown, which billowed from the skirting board like water damage. Aware of the surprising deliberation that Wetherspoons puts into its carpet commissions, I wondered if this ectoplasmic design was a reference to the Yarborough's spooky past or an evocation of the area's aquatic heritage.*

‖‖

* *Spoon's Carpets* by Kit Caless reveals the consideration that goes into the chain's bespoke carpet designs, which are harmonised with the historical buildings in which they are laid, reflecting the stories of their past or the idiosyncrasies of the architecture. Examples include a mineshaft motif in the Spoons of a former colliery town, art deco stylings in a restored cinema in Whitstable and postage stamps on the carpet in a former Post Office.

The Lincolnshire seaport of Grimsby sits in marshland on the south bank of the Humber estuary, dominated by a Victorian brick tower that rises from the dock. It used to be one of the world's biggest fishing ports, so busy that it is said you could cross the waters of the dock without getting wet, by walking across the rows of tied-up trawlers. Jobs were plentiful and money from visiting trawlermen poured into the pubs and shops, buoying the local economy. But in the latter half of the twentieth century the fishing industry began to decline, exacerbated by the loss of the 'Cod Wars' to Iceland, and much of the port's heritage architecture was demolished to be replaced with concrete tower blocks, shopping centres and car parks. In 2016, Grimsby was voted the worst place to live in Britain, while the Royal Society of Public Health ranked its high street as the unhealthiest in the country, thanks to the prevalence of bookmakers, off-licences, fast-food joints and empty shops. It is safe to say, then, that Grimsby is not a go-to tourist destination for those seeking scenic views and boutique shops. Unlike gothic Whitby, eighty miles north, with its ruined abbey, craggy cliffs and associations with Bram Stoker's *Dracula,* it is not a famed hub of spectres, demons and monsters. But that is not to say Grimsby is without its ghosts; it's just that you won't find them drifting down cobbled lanes or lurking in Victorian villas. Instead, as I was to discover that night, they can be found in its modern council estates.

After I dumped my bags at the hotel, I stepped out into the evening. Behind the station was the Duchess Street car park, almost empty. Street lamps cast an orange haze on the tarmac as I made my way along the fence beside the train tracks. A sign bolted onto the slats asked arriving rail workers ARE YOU FIT FOR THE DUTIES YOU WILL BE UNDERTAKING TODAY?, presumably in the hope it would strike home with someone too drunk, stoned or disturbed to operate heavy machinery. Quite frankly, if I felt mentally under the weather, the suspicion that a sentient fence was speaking directly to me might send me over the edge. At the eastern side of the car park was a maintenance depot, doors opened, hisses and clangs coming from within. The building was clad in wooden panels that had become weathered, the green paint peeling. That's when it caught my eye: the face of a middle-aged man staring out from a patch of exposed plywood, his brow heavy, jaw grizzled, cheekbones sunken. I blinked and looked again. It was unmistakably a human face, sepia-toned and blurred as if photographed with an old camera. With a shiver, I put it down to pareidolia and hurried down Railway Terrace towards my destination.

I had arranged to visit Jackie Cheffins, someone I'd known on Twitter for years and a lifelong Grimsby resident. She welcomed me into the living room of her Victorian terrace house, where a fire crackled and the John Cusack disaster film *2012* played out quietly on the TV. 'California is going down,' Cusack yelled into his phone as he barrelled down the freeway in a limousine. Jackie handed me a beer and we talked for a while about our lives while in the background flyovers, tower blocks and restaurants were swallowed up by an earth that was being rent asunder. I told Jackie about my book project and asked if there was any local weirdness of which I should be aware. 'I can't think of anything in particular,' she said, handing me a cocktail to go with my beer, 'except the thing with the Christmas tree.' The Norwegian fir erected by the council in the town centre that December was so threadbare that it was removed after protests from locals. In its place someone had placed a miniature Christmas tree, about shin high, in ludicrous disproportion to the barriers around it. The townsfolk wanted to keep it even after a new tree was installed. 'That's the sort of thing we find funny,' Jackie said.

A little while later, her friend Rachel turned up and sat by the fire as we awaited a taxi to take us to the pub. After I told her why I was in Grimsby, Jackie asked, 'Can you think of anything?'

'No, I don't think so,' Rachel frowned. On the TV screen a light aircraft carrying John Cusack and his family took off from a disintegrating runway and soared between two collapsing skyscrapers as Los Angeles tilted into the Pacific Ocean. 'Actually . . . come to think of it, there was one thing. A guy who lived on the estate near me was haunted by a nun, so he set up a ghostbusting team. They'd drive around town with a giant dog investigating supernatural events.'

'Oh yeah,' said Jackie. 'I'd forgotten about that.'

I was gobsmacked. Imagine living in a town so eccentric that its residents could forget about the time when it had its own Ghostbusters. But when I later researched the story, I discovered that it was utterly true – or at least as true as a ghostbusting story can be.

The housing estate Rachel referred to is called Nunsthorpe. It took its name from a twelfth-century nunnery, the Priory of St Leonard, which was dissolved by Henry VIII in 1539, subsequently becoming a farm for four centuries. The Nunsthorpe estate was built in the 1920s and 1930s, driven by a need to provide new homes for returning servicemen after the First World War.

In the early 1980s, a businessman named Robin Furman lived in a house on Nun's Corner, north-east of the estate. One evening as he was going upstairs, he saw a nun on the landing, dressed in her habit. At first she appeared to be human but, as he approached, he realised that she had no face. Before he could scrutinise her further, she vanished. With a lifelong interest in parapsychology, Furman was fascinated rather than frightened by the apparition and the incident inspired him to complete a degree in psychology and philosophy. After he graduated, he lectured at local colleges and took on local paranormal cases as part of his research. To aid him, he recruited friends and relatives including a microbiologist, a photographer, a computer consultant, an electronics engineer and his son Andy. Together they became the Grimsby Ghostbusters. Their call-out vehicle was a 1959 Austin Princess, a former mayoral limousine, and their weapon of choice was the Roboghost, an electronic detection machine constructed from an Acorn computer. The Ghostbusters were often accompanied by Furman's 14-stone

Newfoundland dog, Ben – adding a Scooby-Doo twist to the Ghostbusters theme.

After Furman's team arrived at a haunted location, they would take temperature readings to detect spirits, then use chalk markings, rope and cardboard pyramids to create a 'ring of power' to repel malignant forces. These methods seemed to work and the Grimsby Ghostbusters were recruited to deal with a slew of supernatural jobs in the locale. Their cases included a semi-detached home where a woman was possessed by an ancient Sumerian demonic entity named Pazuzu; a car auction house in Cleethorpes haunted by a man who had hanged himself in the ghost-train ride of the theme park that used to occupy the site; and a haunted shoe shop on Wellowgate in Grimsby, where the manageress had seen an elderly fellow in Rupert Bear trousers and a woolly jumper walk between the aisles then vanish through a wall, leaving a smell of tobacco behind him. Afterwards, the staff reported recurring incidents of items being moved from the racks and unseen fingers tickling customers' feet when they were trying on shoes. And then there was the case of a flat above a dress shop, where disembodied voices called the occupants' names and the apparition of a 'yellow man' was seen staring from the window. This shop, it turns out, is just across the road from the Duchess Street car park, where I had encountered that sepia-toned face on the side of the depot on my first night in the town.

Most of the cases investigated by the Grimsby Ghostbusters occurred in modern, unassuming buildings, particularly in the town's housing estates. But why might this be? After all, spectres are usually associated with places deeply layered with history, which is why we tend to associate hauntings with Edwardian, Victorian, Georgian or Tudor houses. Robin Furman's theory is that supernatural occurrences are caused by the emotions of living beings in the here and now rather than ghosts from the past or spirits from another dimension. He believes that these apparitions are 'thought forms' created in the mind of the disturbed resident which afterwards gain their own independent energy. In his book *Ghostbusters UK: A Casebook of Hauntings and Exorcisms*, co-written with journalist Moira Martingale, Furman explains:

> Reality is a very fragile thing. It can change from fraction of a second to fraction of a second, so things you create in your own mind can develop a reality just as powerful, maybe more powerful than the apparently solid table that you see in front of you.[10]

Furman reasoned that the only way to banish the offending 'spirits' was to convince the victims of the hauntings that his rituals and sigils were effective – and to believe it himself. This mutual bond of belief could effect a real change in the energies of the room and release the household from the grip of the thought form.

In one case he visited a semi-detached council house where a young couple lived with their twenty-one-month-old baby. They were plagued by the sound of footsteps on the landing and the lights switching on and off at night. One day they returned home to discover a ransacked back bedroom, but with no sign of burglary. A neighbour later told them that he had spotted an old man's face in the window earlier that day, which led them to suspect the ghost might be Ben Foster, an elderly man who had lived in the house before them until he died of cancer. But Robin Furman had a different theory; he suspected that strains in the couple's marriage were causing a manifestation of bad energy. He describes the bedroom that had been ransacked as being full of photos of scantily clad women and motorcycle equipment from the husband's 'footloose and fancy-free days'. When confronted about it, the wife confided that they had split up recently, and that the hauntings had temporarily stopped, only to resume when the husband returned to the family home. Furman wondered if it was resentment about his behaviour that caused a 'vortex of power which destroyed the room'.[11]

When viewed from this perspective, there is no reason why a twentieth-century terraced house on a council estate cannot be as racked with emotional energies as a sixteenth-century Tudor cottage. A suburban housing estate, with its identikit houses, arranged in neat rows and grids, belies the uniqueness of every situation behind each closed door, where all kinds of deeply complex narrative can unfold. The personality clashes. The erotic awakenings. The teenage angst. The failing marriages. The relationship betrayals. The tragic deaths. Sometimes the present can haunt the living as much as the past.

Grimsby struggled in the 1970s as the town hit hard times. Without a thriving fishing industry, the community was deprived of its core reason for existing and became blighted by crime and social disorder. This must have cast a pall of uncertainty, stress and anxiety on many of the inhabitants, so perhaps it is not a coincidence that it was during this same period of decline that many of the supernatural disturbances on the Nunsthorpe Estate occurred. For instance, in 1977, John and Doreen Routledge, who lived on Caistor Drive with their four children, found themselves being pushed, kicked and punched by an invisible entity inside their home. The campaign of harassment began with inexplicably rumpled bed sheets, which they blamed on the family dog, until they shut him in the scullery one day and returned home to find the same mess in the bedroom. Knocks and bangs regularly startled the family. Items would go missing. Doreen would lay out clothes for the kids and then find them neatly arranged in the wardrobe. On one occasion the spirit threw a towel on the scullery floor in front of her and she was so fed up by this point that she sharply admonished it. When she later returned to the room, the towel was hanging up neatly on the rail. Their twelve-year-old daughter Carol claimed to have seen the culprit, describing it as red-eyed, black and 'with sort of spikes around its head'. And Doreen described the feeling of coming into contact with it: 'When it touches you it is really cold, like touching a dead person, and sometimes when it is about there is a terrible smell.'

Eventually, the Reverend Fred Grossmith carried out an exorcism and the disturbances stopped. But this wasn't the only haunting on the estate. At a house on Langton Drive in the 1980s Sharon Grenny's family was tormented by the apparition of a monk who, just like Robin Furman's nun, had no face. It once appeared at the end of her bed and again on the stairs in front of her daughter. They became so frightened that they successfully convinced the council to rehome them.[12] Bearing in mind the deep religious history of the Priory, which came long before the estate, were the nun and the monk examples of Furman's 'thought forms' or were they spectres of what lay beneath the bricks and tarmac?

As can be expected in a cramped island, many housing estates in Britain are built on land with former uses. The Byker Estate in Newcastle-upon-Tyne is near the location of Hadrian's Wall, and was once home to garrisons of Roman soldiers. The Gurnos Estate in Merthyr Tydfil, South Wales, was built on woodland and farmland that included the Goitre Pond, notorious for suicides and drownings. The Admirals Way housing estate in Andover, Hampshire, was built on an area of waste ground used by travellers; long before that, in 1890 when it was farmland, someone was hanged there at a site known as the Drunken Tree. Some estates have been built on former aerodromes, lidos, school playing fields and industrial land. Many of London's modern estates were placed on the sites of Victorian slums, high-rises pushing up from the dust and debris of millions of forgotten personal histories.

The modern housing estate is often a continuation of a much older story.

Sometimes that story can haunt the present. In 1975, for example, a TV crew for the programme *Nationwide* visited a newly built housing block in Battle Hill, Wallsend, to investigate reports that it was haunted. Since the day they had moved in, Kathy Gallon and her family had been disturbed by footsteps and bangs on the wall of their maisonette. They had become so scared that they decamped each night to her mother's house. Other residents complained about sudden rushes of cold wind and inexplicable thuds from unoccupied rooms. The TV crew spent a night there and heard nothing, but the sound technician later ventured an explanation for what was going on. The block of flats had been 'floated on a raft' over a former coal mine, and the flimsy plasterboard of the structure was acting as an amplifier. The location's industrial past was quite literally rising up from the earth and rattling the walls of its present-day occupants. More recently, in 2016, residents of the Bayfield Estate, North Tyneside, were evacuated after severe subsidence damage, caused by the collapse of shallow coalmines beneath their homes. In those first inexplicable, shifting moments, I wonder if any of those residents felt a glimmer of fear that something supernatural was occurring.

Buildings are always connected to the past; they are made from ancient materials hewn from beneath our feet. In her astonishing biography of British landscape, *A Land*, Jacquetta Hawkes takes the reader on a journey from the formation of the planet, through the geological upheavals that created what we know as Britain today, to the time in which she was writing, 1949, on the pivot of a rapidly changing century. She described how Cambrian mud formed the Welsh slates used for roofs; how Jurassic rocks were crucial to the Bath and Portland stone structures of the eighteenth century; and how Carboniferous sandstones defined the buildings of the Victorian era. These diverse stones, filled with fossils, ancient plants and antediluvian sediments, were what gave Britain's urban areas their distinct regional differences. Hawkes lamented the new materials of glass, steel and cheap composite bricks, interpreting them as a sign that we were being cut off from the land. 'A house at Bradford, a house at Dagenham,' she wrote, 'will show the same silly stucco, the same paltry composition roof.' She added that the housing estates emerging on the outskirts of cities were 'a limbo created by the combination of meanness with theoretical good intentions'.[13]

When you read the rousing prose of *A Land*, it is hard not to feel keenly that difference between old buildings, with the sweep of geological history ingrained in their fabric, and modern houses, which can seem tawdry and soulless by comparison. However, the experience of the residents of the new-build maisonettes in Wallsend belies this idea. The whooshes, slams and bangs that terrified them in 1975 were an effect of deep pits bored in the earth to dig out the carbonised remnants of 300-million-year-old tropical forests. Whether they realised it or not, they were as connected to the land as anyone living in a sandstone house or walking on marble tiles. But even for the vast majority of housing estates that aren't built on booming mine shafts, the same applies. It is not the physical properties of the things we feel connected to that are important, but the act of connection itself – even if it is to plywood, UPVC and that grey pebbledash of the first house in which I lived, which so fascinated me as a little kid.

Today's building materials might be synthetic, rather than accumulations of magma, dead forests and marine animals, but their ingredients remain of this earth, and their usage is the result of the accumulation of human knowledge since we first stood on two legs. I agree that we need to remain in touch with the land but it doesn't have to be via ancient stone or what we usually call 'nature'. It could be through the tiny cryptoforests that flourish in verges of roads and cracks in paving stones; the miraculous textures of concrete and glass; the sounds of shrieking urban foxes; or the smell of hot tarmac. Anybody should be able to feel a connection with place, no matter where they grew up or where they live, even in the densest concrete jungles or the most monotonous suburban sprawls. Any material can become a repository for memory once it becomes saturated with life and death, love and loss. Any place, no matter how mundane, can resonate with meaning. There can be as much poetry in housing estates – so new in Hawkes's time but weathered in the decades since, physically and emotionally – as there is in the Jurassic limestone of a London cathedral.

|||||||||||||||

With at least three publicly reported hauntings on one estate, and possibly more that were never recorded, I had to visit the Nunsthorpe Estate in Grimsby to scope it out for myself, even if the likelihood of meeting phantom monks and nuns was virtually nil. I wanted to find out if there was any intrinsic quality to the place that might suggest why it was the haunt of ghosts and poltergeists. It was twilight when I parked up on Caistor Drive, the location of the first spectre. Beneath a bruised December sky, slate roofs shimmered, the silent streets slung with telephone wires. Behind hedgerows the spidery arms of trees were raised in a frozen panic. The roads curved and intersected in graceful arcs, forming – when viewed from above on Google Earth – what looks like an inverted arched window. There were no yellow markings or white lines. Only modern cars and satellite dishes made the scene any different from how it would have appeared during the 1970s and 1980s. On the corner of an end-terrace, a garden with swings, slide and trampoline. Two narrow windows stared dolefully out from the side of the house. I heard the chatter of voices from a muffled TV but there was not a single person in view. This huge housing estate was unusually lacking in visible signs of human life, but I could sense hidden energies at play beneath the surface.

At the top of Langton Drive, the site of the second poltergeist incident, stood the Nunsthorpe Tavern, its empty car park barriered by a metal link chain with spikes, echoing little Carol Routledge's description of the spiky-headed phantom. Adjacent was a row of shops, outside which the bollards were tilted as if

View of the pub car park on Langton Drive.

a beast had gone berserk. Behind it was a patch of wasteland, strewn with flaps of cardboard and white carrier bags that shivered in the breeze. The sign for Langton Drive was badly rusted, while the sign for the pub, creaking on a pole by the road, was blank: a totally white space overlooking an empty car park. An estate agency billboard on the wall read: COULD YOU RUN THIS PUB? It made me assume that the place had closed down until I saw a figure in its doorway, cast in the glow of an external security light, smoking a cigarette. His facial features weren't visible, and he didn't move as I crossed beneath the blank pub sign, though I was certain that he was watching me. Perhaps he was not of this world. As Robin Furman says in his book: 'It makes you wonder how many times people meet ghosts and don't even realise it.'[14]

I was fully aware that my perspective was under the influence of stories about dissolved priories, faceless nuns, disturbed monks and poltergeists. What I had read about Nunsthorpe had fermented in my imagination to produce these sensations, intensified by expectation and enchanted by a chilly December twilight at the thinning of the day. But isn't this how we experience a place? For a place is more than bricks and mortar. More than a map. More than a bunch of articles about social deprivation and sneery lists of Britain's worst towns. A place is made of stories you read and rumours you hear. It is made of prejudices and anxieties, shaped by your past experiences. It is an atmosphere – a synchronicity of light, sound, smell, texture and temperature. It is a memory triggered in the deep recesses of your subconscious. A horror from your past. An anxiety in your present. A desire for your future. It is a projection of your state of mind, which can make manifest the invisible, animate the inanimate, and imbue even the dullest modern house with a sinister energy.

The artist Marc Renshaw once told me a story about a time when he was six years old, playing with his friend Terry on a field near his home on the Isle of Man. They were looking at a cluster of buildings in the far distance, beyond a building site, when Terry pointed out one that he said was haunted. He had seen mysterious red lights moving around it after dark. Following the trajectory of his friend's finger, Marc's gaze settled on a modern five-bedroom property on the skyline. From that day forth, it became known as 'the haunty', a place that Marc feared intensely. He would get a chill just looking at it. Whenever he and Terry talked of the haunty, that was the house Marc thought about. It was only many years later that Marc found out Terry had not been referring to the modern townhouse at all but to a crumbling cottage next to it, which Marc had simply not spotted. He had imbued the wrong house with sinister qualities purely because he misread the direction of his friend's finger. But why might a modern townhouse not seem menacing to a young mind that has not yet been indoctrinated into the aesthetics of horror?

It reminds me of a passage in *Walking's New Movement* by Phil Smith, a writer, academic researcher and performer who specialises in mythogeography, a method of reinterpreting and enchanting everyday experience. He describes how he grew up on a road of newly built suburban houses in which he found plenty to tantalise his mind as an intrepid young adventurer: 'Trails opened up across multiple gardens,' he writes, 'offering us imaginary, social and, later, sexual playgrounds where a couple of rows of loganberries passed for a wilderness, a pear tree for a forest, a Himalayan Balsam for a Triffid, a coal bunker for a confessional, a shed for a pyramid to be grave robbed.' As Phil explains, it didn't matter that these objects and places weren't old, rustic or considered natural. Children can find gaps in the humdrum world around them that are 'explorable and trespassable, connective and ambiguous'.[15]

I know from my own experience that there can be something unsettling about rows of unassuming, duplicate buildings beyond well-trimmed hedges, where anything could happen behind closed doors. I grew up in a semi-detached townhouse in a suburban 1960s estate on the northern edge of Glossop, in Derbyshire. The garage was built into the house, with white wooden slats around the bottom floor and honeycombed tiles beneath the bedroom windows. At the time we moved in, the house was only fifteen years old. There were no period features inside. No fireplace. No dado rails. No cornices. Only smooth walls, low ceilings, plain brown carpets and double-glazed patio doors. But there was plenty to frighten a kid with a big imagination. For one thing, I refused to sleep with my back to the bedroom door or dangle a foot over the side of the bed in case I might feel a cold hand grab my foot. Occasionally I played a game of terror by turning off the light on the landing and then tearing down the stairs through the blackness in a race against demons I could not see, heart in my throat. For a child, the physical world is open to constant interpretation, and any object can contain multiple values at the same time. Stairs are stairs, but they are also a mountainside, which can turn into a waterfall, sluicing you to your doom in the hallway, which might be a lake of crocodiles or a pit of molten lava. To me, our house was a castle. A spaceship. An alien planet. A TARDIS.

Our road, Cedar Close, was a quiet street of identikit houses with rectangular gardens and cars parked on sloped drives. There was a parallel road called Spinney Close where my friend lived, which was an exact replica of ours; playing in his house felt like being in my home but in some other dimension. There was strangeness beneath the genteel exteriors. Next door lived a woman who never left the house. All I ever saw was the odd glimpse of her inside her house, staring from the kitchen window as I set off on my bike, her expression inscrutable, but in my imagination terrifying: her fanged teeth bared in a silent scream of fury. There was a sparse line of shrubs separating her lawn from ours, which meant our football would often roll through into her garden. My brother and I would dare each other to go and retrieve it, knowing that she'd be watching us. I don't remember precisely why we were so scared. We had never really seen her in the flesh, forcing us to construct her in our minds, based on the kind of adult who would never leave their house – a concept incomprehensible to me as a boy who liked to spend most of his time outdoors. I remember my mum saying something about 'agoraphobia', but I didn't know what it meant. Whatever the reasons for her self-exile, I just assumed that they were monstrous.

At the top of the close, in a house on the corner, lived an old man who I would see from time to time. I didn't think anything of him at first. Old people who were not my grandparents had little interest for me. So I was surprised to see him walk into our classroom at school one afternoon, smiling benevolently. He was a writer, the teacher said, and he was going to tell us the story of Howard Carter, Lord Carnarvon and the Egyptian Pharaoh Tutankhamun. As the old man spoke, I was enraptured by of the story of the boy king's cursed tomb, and the deaths that subsequently befell those who had intruded on his resting place. From then on, whenever I rode past his house I'd assume it was full of amulets, stone tablets and dusty old papyrus manuscripts, as if he was Derbyshire's aged answer to Indiana Jones.

Around the same time, I remember watching an episode of the American TV show *Hart to Hart*, about the wealthy husband-and-wife crime-fighting duo Jonathan and Jennifer Hart. In 'Murder Wrap', they were investigating the case of an Egyptologist allegedly killed by an ancient mummified Egyptian prince in search of his beloved princess, who happened to look like Jennifer. In one scene, the mummy appeared in her window and in another a dog-headed statue came to life and attacked them. I was eight years old and it was one of the scariest things I'd ever seen. Cursed mummies shot high up on my list of fears along with nuclear bombs, sharks and Triffids. At night, I lay in bed and worried about the many terrifying things that could lurk outside our house, imagining legions of monsters from film and TV shambling across the patio.

When I was twelve I wrote these fears into a story entitled 'Outside my Window', about a boy who couldn't get to sleep on a stormy night, convinced he could hear scratching and snuffling in the garden. Downstairs, his parents were watching TV with the volume up loud, so they hadn't heard anything and when the boy went downstairs to plead with his parents to look, they were too engrossed in their programme to bother.

Besides, this was just another one of his tall tales and they were sick of them. 'It's just the storm,' they insisted. 'Go back to bed.' But back in his room he could hear it climbing the wall outside, getting closer and closer, until it began to rattle the window. The boy forced himself to find out once and for all what was out there. It probably was just the wind and rain. He was imagining things again. That must be it. So he slid from his bed and stepped across the soft carpet to his venetian blinds. He took a deep breath, grabbed the cord, and pulled. The blinds flipped open. Lightning flashed. The boy, shrieking in terror, was confronted by the deformed visage of a slimy egg-headed alien, pressed against the glass, screaming back at him.

I never considered relocating my story to a cabin in the woods, or a remote cottage on a moor. What scared me was the idea that in the supposed safety of my everyday world, menacing entities might lurk from which even my parents couldn't protect me. There was no reason for these beings to wish me harm. They just did, which is what made it even more frightening. Looking back, the writing of that story coincided with the time I left my primary school and experienced a huge health scare; a medical examination ended up with me in hospital being checked for a suspected heart murmur. During an ultrasound I was forced to watch, aghast, as my heart pulsed on a monitor like the slimy-faced alien blob I'd imagined outside my bedroom window. The story was about losing the sanctuary of childhood innocence; the realisation that bad things could happen outside anyone's control; and that nowhere was truly safe. If the enemy could exist even inside my own body, then it could certainly be inside my house.

\|\|\|\|\|\|\|\|\|\|\|\|\|\|\|\|\|\|\|

The collision between peaceful suburban setting and horrifying phenomenon has so fully entered the popular folk conscious-ness that the modern terrace council house is now synonymous with poltergeists. One thing these stories have in common is that they consistently involve families with children, particu-larly around the age of twelve. It is as if pre-pubescence is a lightning rod for the demonic or, as the likes of Robin Furman might suggest, a telekinetic cause of the mayhem.

The most famous example in Britain occurred in the London suburb of Enfield in 1977. The Hodgson family, residents of an unremarkable semi-detached council house, was terrorised by an entity that hurled objects across the room. During a police visit, a chair slid across the floor, with no evidence of trickery found. The identity of the phantom was suspected to be Bill Wilkins, a cantankerous old man who had died in the house years earlier. Speaking through the apparently possessed eleven-year-old Janet Hodgson, Bill explained: 'I went blind, and then I had an 'aemorrhage and I fell asleep and I died in the chair in the corner downstairs.' The story made the global news after a *Daily Mirror* photographer, Graham Morris, took a picture of Janet levitating in her bedroom. A TV series, *The Enfield Haunting,* later reimagined the events, followed by the Hollywood film *The Conjuring 2.*

74

A similar case that took place at the end of the 1960s also ended up being turned into a horror film – underlining the way that modern 'history-less' settings have gradually seeped into our folklore. In this case the Pritchard family had moved into a three-bedroom, semi-detached council house in Pontefract, West Yorkshire. Shortly afterwards, parents Jean and Joe embarked on a holiday with their daughter, leaving their teenage son Philip at home with his grandmother. On a warm summer day, Philip rushed in from the garden to get some water, when a gust of icy wind slammed the door behind him. As he carried his drink into the living room, he was perplexed to see a fine white powder falling from the ceiling above where his grandmother was standing. In the kitchen they were shocked to find puddles of water pooling on the floor. They made a call to the Water Board who hunted the property for leaks but found nothing. Later that evening, they were startled by a sudden crash, and discovered a plant from the hallway now standing halfway up the stairs. When cups began to rattle on the shelves they fled to a neighbour's house. There were no more incidents until two years later, when the suspected poltergeist resumed its exploits with gusto. Bangs on the walls. Broken crockery. Drops in temperature. Weird smells. Green foam erupting from taps. Shoves in the back.

Refusing to be bullied out of their home, the Pritchards decided to evict their guest, who they named 'Fred', through exorcisms, to which he reacted by slapping faces and daubing upside-down crosses on the walls. Events reached a terrifying peak when their young daughter Diane was dragged upstairs by her throat. Eventually, Fred made himself visible at the foot of Joe and Jean Pritchard's bed: a tall figure in black robes. From this, paranormal investigator Tom Cuniff later ascertained that Fred was the ghost of a Cluniac monk who had been hanged for raping and murdering a young girl in the seventeenth century. The house was not only situated near to where the gallows pole would have been, but beneath the living room was a well down which the body of the monk had been thrown after his death.

This is what happens if you scratch beneath the tarmac of British estates. There are few parts of this island not trampled by feet, spilled with blood, or marked by stories, even if they have been long forgotten. All we know are the recorded usages of a piece of land, recent fragments of a story reaching back to the last Ice Age. Our suburban estates are perched on dark icebergs of history we shall never know, but which we might sense occasionally, when the walls shake and voices cry out.

The case of the Black Monk of Pontefract not only inspired the 2012 horror film *When the Lights Went Out* – directed by Pat Holden, nephew of Jean Pritchard – it also led to the transformation of a council house into a tourist attraction. The producer of the film, Bill Bungay, bought the property but never moved in, instead reinstating the 1970s furniture and decor and turning it into a guesthouse. On his website Bungay warns: '30 East Drive, Pontefract, IS NOT a traditional guesthouse, Hotel, B&B or party venue – and the owner recommends that you DO NOT visit.' He also calls attention to continued supernatural occurrences at the property such as the 'fairly recent occasion' when 'the bed in the small room was trashed by the poltergeist during a 3 a.m. loss of temper'. He advises guests to 'please bear this in mind when deciding to spend the night in this particular room'.

Despite these warnings – or, more likely, because of these warnings – the house is a popular draw for ghost hunters, with constant bookings all year round. Guests report bumps in the night, feelings of nausea and unusual smells. Keys are stolen. Marbles are thrown. Shadowy figures glimpsed in the corner of rooms. In 2016, ghost hunter Pete Boulton caught what might have been the Black Monk of Pontefract's face staring from a mirror – an entity with the beard and hair of ELO frontman Jeff Lynne. That same year, Claire Cowell from the East Drive Paranormal Group captured the image of a black-clad arm clutching rosary beads. And in 2019 Jason Whitnell took a photo that appears to show the figure of a child staring from the doorway, suggesting that it is not only Fred who haunts the house but a menagerie of ghosts. The property on East Drive has been transformed from an unremarkable council house into a powerful conduit for the imagination, with the narrative expanding from the angry monk to new personalities, with fresh suggestions of what might lurk within. Whether based on a hoax or not, the popularity of this house illustrates a shift in the locus of hauntings from ostensibly 'old' buildings to structures of the late twentieth century. The Enfield and Pontefract events take place in mundane properties, which means what happens within their walls could happen to anyone.

Inside East Drive's living room is a stone-effect fireplace, Artex wall, brown side table, green sofa and anodyne framed landscape painting. The decor deepens the resonance of the horror for generations who grew up with these colours, textures, styles and artefacts in the 1960s and 1970s. Those decades haunt us not only because of rampaging poltergeists, but because they define the past experience of a generation who grew up in these places, now aged in their forties, fifties and sixties. Many are the writers, TV producers, comedians and artists who are telling stories and commissioning works today.

Jane Samuels is one such artist. Her work is based on urban exploration with a particular interest in the concept of trespass. One of her favourite sites was a terraced Victorian house on Rochdale Road in Manchester, which had lain unoccupied since the 1970s. An art teacher who had worked with prisoners in Risley and Strangeways prisons, Jane first learnt about the property from some former inmates who used it to take drugs.* It was completely sealed up, so the only way she could enter was through a hole in the backyard, which allowed her to drop down into the pitch-black basement. 'I spent a couple of

---

* 'A form of local folklore builds up around drug houses,' says Jane Samuels. 'There is a degree of pride in being part of the drug counterculture – living outside of the norm – with your own language and culture. It has a bearing on where people go, what they do, how they speak and how they behave. Their stories are sometimes violent, sometimes very sad, and completely normalised. This makes the places in which they hang out become all of those things.'

minutes keeping very still,' she said, 'just listening and thinking, is there anyone down here, or up there above me?' She could hear shuffling and scratching. Pigeons or rats, but she could not be sure. Once she got her bearings, she picked her way through the darkness and found the steps to the ground floor. This level was the domain of addicts, and she came across a couple of people sitting listlessly, unbothered by her arrival. The users never left the ground floor so when she climbed the stairs she discovered a perfectly preserved time capsule from the 1970s, with period wallpaper, furnishings and ornaments. There were markings on the walls where clocks had once hung. Tins of NHS milk lined the shelves. Family photos were propped up on the mantelpiece. In a bedroom, she found children's toys, a ticket for the January 1975 match between Manchester United and Norwich City, and a door covered in Sellotaped football cards showing the top players of the era.

'I was taken straight back in time to my grandad's house in Salford in the 1970s,' Jane said. 'It felt visceral – very real and powerfully familiar. There was something so instantly evocative about this house. It hit me hard. I can only describe it as a form of haunting.'

This is a fascinating twist on the classic ghost stories I remember as a child in the 1970s, in which Victorian-era ghosts in Victorian-era houses menaced those in the present. In this case, the Victorian house that Jane had entered was being haunted but by the ghosts of lives lived there in the 1970s. One of her most affecting finds was a black and white photo of a dog standing on its hind legs, taken in the backyard of the same house. The shadow of the owner is cast against the wall behind the dog – the ghostly outline of a woman in a dress, at whom the dog stares in devotion. It is a fragment of a joyful life experienced by a person or persons unknown in a time long gone. 'The power of an object like that stops you dead,' says Jane. 'It sucks all the air out of a room.' She returned to the house numerous times before it was sold for development, trying to soak it all in before it was gone. But what Jane was yearning for wasn't the Victorian architecture, nor the 1970s memorabilia, but the memories of her past that the house activated: its smells, colours and sensations allowing her to time travel to her childhood, where she could see her grandfather in the backroom, tending to his tomatoes. This might have been a dilapidated crack house but it was also what she describes as 'a deeply transcendent entity: a portal' and one that was about to be closed off forever.

The East Drive property in Pontefract is a similar portal, a time capsule – albeit one fabricated for the benefit of tourists. The owner's recreation of a shabby, unstylish 1970s interior doesn't just transport the visitor back to the origins of the poltergeist event; it enhances the ghostliness for anyone who experienced that decade, triggering feelings of melancholy and nostalgia; thoughts of loved ones we lost; pieces of ourselves that we miss.

||||||||||||||||||

These stories illustrate how the spectres of the second half of the twentieth century have begun to haunt both its structures and our imaginations, but in the 1980s, signs of a new kind of haunting emerged in the housing estates and tower blocks of Britain. This time it wasn't the loss of the past that tormented people, but the loss of a future. After Thatcher's election in 1979, Britain experienced seismic shifts from nationalised industry to privatised capital, with sustained attacks on regulation and the welfare state. While this made many financiers and speculators very wealthy, it also caused deprivation in those communities whose fates were inextricably tied to the old industries of mining, steel and shipbuilding.

The television play *Govan Ghost Story*, broadcast in 1989, is set in the Iona Court high-rise in Govan, Glasgow, as the city struggles in the grip of a recession. The shipbuilding days are over and Jock, a former activist in the fight to protect the industry, lives alone in his flat, embittered by the past and unable to come to terms with what has happened to the city. To his dismay, his estranged daughter is about to marry a Thatcherite yuppie who lives in a new high-rise with security and glass doors, while his tower block is decayed and graffitied. Jock is haunted by the apparition of a small girl who appears in the hallway outside his flat. Crashes, shouts and cries assail him from the empty property next door. As he delves deeper, he discovers that a violent father threw his daughter to her death from the balcony of that flat, and it is her ghost that appears to him. Feeling guilty for neglecting his own daughter during the struggle for the shipyards, Jock sees a parallel between the murderer and himself. The absence of his daughter from his life is a loss that might have been prevented but for the economic catastrophe with which he felt he had to contend.

As M. J. Steel Collins points out in her article about the play on the Spooky Isles website, the location of Jock's flat was once the site of Boomloan House, known to local kids as 'the Hunty', because of rumoured ghost sightings there.[16] On the face of it, then, *Govan Ghost Story* is in a similar vein to the real-life events in Enfield, Pontefract and the Nunsthorpe estate, where the building is haunted not only by a recent tragedy that took place within its walls, but also by echoes of the past before its construction. However, *Govan Ghost Story* is more than a tale of the supernatural. It is about how economic and industrial decline can haunt the present with the spectre of an aborted future. Jock is full of regret about his life while the tower block itself is affected psychically by the tragedies of neglect and social deprivation that scar its relatively recent history. Iona High Court was designed to be a fresh architectural start after the horrors of the Second World War, but in the play it has become a symptom of the state's failure to look after the poorest and most needy in society in the wake of catastrophic economic decline. The utopian vision of low-cost communal housing in the sky quickly became a nightmare of design faults, poor construction, underfunding and unsupervised communal spaces rife with crime. The late cultural critic Mark Fisher described the concept of eeriness as 'something present where there should be nothing' or 'nothing present when there should be something'.[17] By his latter definition, a tower block can become eerie in the absence of that life it once promised.

This applies to many of those pioneering residential estates that appeared in Britain's new towns after the Second World War, including Crawley, Harlow and Stevenage. In the new town of Basildon, Essex, the Five Links Estate was designed in the late 1960s as a series of interlinking corridors and courtyards, without roads, so that children could play freely with no traffic to worry about. Those who grew up there in the 1970s and 1980s have fond memories of racing around on their Choppers, interacting with the other kids on the estate, enjoying the green spaces. However, right from the beginning, locals nicknamed the place 'Alcatraz', after the notorious San Francisco prison, because of its maze of stark avenues with blind corners, which could become intimidating at night. The estate was never endowed with a community centre or pub and began to suffer the effects of those cuts to investment which were happening across Basildon.

The town lost its parks, its free sports equipment and those music clubs which once played host to synthesiser bands in the wake of local success story Depeche Mode. Any service deemed costly or unprofitable was scrapped, disintegrating the bonds that were supposed to link people together. After Thatcher launched the Right to Buy scheme, residents quickly began to sell off their properties, further eroding community cohesion. Successive governments since did nothing to reverse this trend and austerity measures after the 2008 banking crash only added to the neglect. When the original vision for an innovative housing estate is considered no longer valid, desirable or properly funded, then the purpose for which it was designed and built no longer exists either, rendering it dysfunctional, left to exist in a cancelled idea – and not because of the failings of its residents, but because of their political abandonment.*

A 2014 YouTube video by former local Stuart Wilson takes a tour around the Five Links Estate, where he fondly remembers playing as a child, now run-down and devoid of any visible human life.[18] His use of spooky synth music and a vintage sepia filter is what might be described as 'hauntological', a term originally coined by the philosopher Jacques Derrida in relation to the spectre of communism, which he claimed was haunting the West even after its collapse. It was a pun on the word 'ontology', the study of being, which sounds like 'hauntology' if you say it in a French accent. His idea was that even something that had not existed or happened can still have a haunting presence. In the 2000s Mark Fisher used the term to describe the way that culture had lost its forward momentum and was folding back on itself, constantly regurgitating existing ideas and art forms, slowly cancelling the future that the twentieth century had led us to expect. Computer technology had dislocated us from

---

* This process of neglect is described in the documentary film about Basildon, *New Town Utopia* (2017), directed by Christopher Ian Smith. As well as portraying the town's decline, the film also depicts a swell of artistic resistance by those who have stayed to tell the story of this unfairly maligned town.

linear time and space, making all information available at once, changing the way we experienced reality, just like in Wilson's film of the Five Links Estate, which digitally manipulates the footage with faux historical effects to enhance the ghostliness of its decayed present, haunted by the absence of what might have been.

In South Wales, the economic problems caused by the decline of mining and steel industries have been so severe that they have led to a new phenomenon – the creation of ghost estates, in which small communities have disappeared, their homes abandoned to nature. Outside Llanelli, the Brynmefys Estate consists of thirty-two properties, but only a couple of them remain inhabited while the rest are home to bats roosting in the rafters. When I paid a visit one summer, it was like walking onto an apocalyptic film set. Weeds burst through tarmac as thistle triffids swayed in former gardens. Creepers consumed the walls of the houses. A pigeon flapped out from a caved-in roof. Security fences lined the road and cut off cul-de-sacs. Some of the windows were boarded up, others smashed. The most disconcerting of them were opened slightly, as if someone had just tried to let air into a stuffy family home. The empty properties had numbers painted on their external walls as if they were prisoners in a camp, awaiting their fate.

But remarkably, one of the houses was inhabited, with a car parked outside. I could see a woman through the kitchen window. The blinds had been raised, net curtains parted, and she was painstakingly cleaning the glass from inside, like an elaborate performance to show the outside world that she was still here, that she was alive and proud of her house, even as the street around her had fallen to ruin. It was incredibly sad. This had once been a neighbourhood, full of life. People mowing their lawns and walking their dogs. The thump of loud music from teenagers' bedrooms. Car engines revving in the mornings. Ice-cream vans in summer. Christmas lights flashing in December. Shrieks of laughter on pissed-up Saturday nights. The rattle and hum of daily existence. All gone, except for this woman, continuing her chores, surrounded by the husks of dead houses. In this estate, the living people are the ghosts.

||||||||||||||||||||

After the devastations of the First and Second World Wars, housing estates spilled out from the cities onto farms, church-owned land, battlefields and ancient woodlands. They covered old wells, lost trackways, execution grounds and mine shafts. In the cities they rose from demolished slums and bombed-out Victorian streets. The narratives they replaced did not all vanish, but continued to make themselves known, from time to time, seeping up from the earth into the consciousness of those young families who were seeking fresh starts in suburbs and commuter belts, away from the chaos of congested cities. For the first decades of their existence these homes were pristine, with all the mod cons of the baby boomer age. Central heating. Double glazing. Utility rooms. Neat little gardens and driveways. They promised an entirely new way of life. But by the end of the 1960s, the dream for some had already begun to sour.

Years of economic decline laid waste to industrial areas, especially in the North, while money flowed from manufacturing into banking and services, for which many people were not skilled, turning instead to poorly paid jobs or unemployment. The suburbs became sites of disaffection, boredom and frustration, while the utopian vision of high-rise living began to fall apart at the seams. This became the era of a new haunted house, modern and unassuming, but tormented with violent energy behind their plain facades, never quite escaping the pull of history, straining with the gravity of life, the loves, the betrayals, the tragedies and deaths. Imaginations cast monsters into the dark corners; heard something frightening in the creaks and groans of new buildings as they settled; sensed all was not right in their ideal home. A nationwide psychic rupture in the 1970s and 1980s saw outbreaks of terror in the cul-de-sacs and avenues of modern estates which have since become enshrined in our contemporary poltergeist mythology.

The true horror of existence is that nightmares follow us, wherever we dwell. Whether it is the troubled married couple on the Nunsthorpe Estate in 1970s Grimsby, the woman alone on a South Wales ghost estate, or my younger self scribbling stories to cope with the end of childhood, what haunts a house is not necessarily the peculiarity of its bricks and mortar, nor the disturbed spirits of those buried beneath its foundations, but ourselves as we struggle to come to terms with the demons in our present.

My house it is on the cold ground,
And oh! Very hard is my past,
But that which troubles me the most is
The unkindness of my guest.
At night he turns my taps on
Then he turns on me,
With slaps about the head so hard
Alack! What remedy?

I cannot see him, but he is there
On Artex walls he scrawls my name
My hopes diminish each day I play
The foul rules of his game
The double-glazing windows rattle,
And bathroom cupboards shake
I know not when the time will come
That my poor mind shall break

There are dead folk 'neath the paving stones
And there's dead folk in the garden
The spectres speak in their ghostly drones,
All beg the lord for pardon
Yet I must endure the tumult still
For there is nowhere else to go
I'm mortgaged right up to the hilt
And the bank manager says 'no'

4

UP IN SMOKE

UNDER THE INFLUENCE OF BREWERIES, FACTORIES AND POWER STATIONS

n 2008 the world plunged into financial crisis. Watching it happen on my TV was like standing in a desert in protective gear witnessing an atomic bomb explode miles away, my face lit by its glow, the mushroom cloud slowly filling my vision. Stock markets fell. Banks were bailed out. The economy spiralled into recession. But I didn't notice any real effect at first. It takes time for the atomic radiation to spread beyond the impact site. The aftershock hit me three years later, when my freelance copywriting contracts started to dry up. Companies were tightening their belts because of falling sales. Letting people go. Doing more work in-house. To exacerbate matters, I had embarked on my first book *Marshland*, a mission that would swallow up most of my time and replace much of my paid work. With accumulating debts, declining income, and a desire to write books, I couldn't afford to live in London. My then-wife and I dreamed of a simpler life by the sea, where we wouldn't have to pedal so hard to keep the cash flowing.

We moved into a near-derelict house in Hastings, East Sussex, which we planned to renovate. As a symbol of my intention to embrace a new landscape on the south coast, I used some of the money from our house sale to buy an artwork that I had been coveting for years: an oil painting of Dungeness Power Station by Bristol-based artist Mark Hollis.

I loved it, even though I had never yet been to Dungeness. Beneath a cloudy blue sky, its brutal grey blocks sitting on a bed of golden yellow. The solidity of the power station contrasted with the dream-like, glitchy quality of its surroundings, as if it was a painting of a memory as much as a place. It was entitled *The Ghost Box*, hinting at its haunted character, but also a reference to Ghost Box records, a label whose artists created eerie analogue synth melodies with fragmented audio clips of 1970s TV, filtered through the sound of crackling vinyl and decaying magnetic tape. One of their albums – *Mind How You Go* by the Advisory Circle – even had a track called 'Nuclear Substation PIF' which ended with a public information film clip that warned, 'KEEP OUT!' Hollis's painting of Dungeness chimed perfectly with the music of Ghost Box Records, filling me with nostalgia for a place I'd never been but hinting at an unnameable terror lurking within those yellow beaches and fluffy clouds.

When we moved to Hastings, I was surprised to discover that it was possible to see the power station from the town on a clear day, even though it was in a different county, twenty miles east. Standing beneath crumbling sandstone cliffs, with my back to the fishing beach, the power station was tiny on the horizon, abstract like Hollis's brutal blocks, seemingly floating on a haze, appearing only on certain days, like an industrial Brigadoon.

Things at home were less inspiring. Our new house was a mouldering wreck of wonky walls, mid-century wiring, lead pipes and damp woodchip partitions from the 1970s. We had to renovate every room, from the bottom up. Despite the carnage, I propped up Hollis's oil painting on a fireplace in the office where I had begun work on a second book, *The Stone Tide*, based on my walks around Hastings. The title was inspired by the phenomenon of longshore drift: the constant eastward dragging of sand and shingle along the south coast of England, intensified by storm tides. Its effects could be devastating. In medieval times, on a pit of shingle less than a mile to the west of where Dungeness stands today, there used to be a thriving town called Old Winchelsea. In the thirteenth century, rising sea levels and storm tides, caused by a prolonged period of warming in the northern hemisphere, ripped the shingle out from underneath the town, sinking it beneath the waves. The entire coastline of East Sussex was reshaped, with ports becoming landlocked, and landlocked towns becoming ports. In 1281 Edward I ordered that a new Winchelsea be built on a hill above what was then a tidal bay, but is now Romney Marsh. But somewhere beneath the sands between Camber and Dungeness lie the bones of the old town – a town that its inhabitants must have thought would exist forever.

The story of Old Winchelsea terrified me, for we live in another period of climate change – a fact brought into sharp focus during my first year in Hastings when a section of the cliff collapsed after months of freakish rainstorms. Beyond the freshly collapsed mounds of rock, Dungeness shimmered on its spit of shingle, now a radioactive time bomb tugged at by longshore drift and threatened by flood. Any disaster that befell the power station would mean the end of my family and everything I knew. I had bought Hollis's painting of the power station because it seemed to symbolise my future on the coast, but now it spoke only of a future disappearing.

Three years into the renovation, the painting was hung beside the fireplace in a finished living room, but those years had taken a heavy toll. Our marriage was over and we had to sell the house we had expected our kids to grow up in. That dream was gone. I was devastated. I had no idea what I was going to do, or where Hollis's painting would next hang. My agonies spilled into the book I was writing, *The Stone Tide*. It was supposed to be about the landscape of East Sussex but had become an auto-fictional account of my personal apocalypse. At its conclusion I fantasised that Dungeness was Avalon, the mythical island where the wounded King Arthur was transported to die. I depicted myself close to death being rowed there on a ghost lifeboat to seek oblivion in the fires that raged in the power station after a lethal storm tide.

I am not the only one to feel this way. In his book about birdwatching in Dungeness, author and Unofficial Britain contributor Gary Budden describes the reactor as 'the power that fuelled the fears of the second half of the twentieth century'. As he searches the stony flatlands for white egrets and other migrating birds, he thinks about filmmaker Derek Jarman's account in his book *Modern Nature* of seeing what he thought was the power station exploding, but was only a lightning strike. Gary wonders if there is a small part of him that also wished to see the station to explode, 'so I could be in the centre of things for one brief, blinding-white moment'.[19]

These fantasies of annihilation I knew well. Dungeness had cast a long, dark shadow over my imagination, which goes to show that buildings can be more than physical structures. They can seep into your thoughts and dreams, with the capacity to haunt you as much as they themselves can be haunted. But what was really chilling about Dungeness Power Station – at least for me – was that the terror came not from past events but from those which had not yet happened.

nnnnnnnnnn

A few years after I imagined my death in Dungeness I met the artist Marc Renshaw in a carvery pub on the fringe of Europarc, outside Grimsby. He had developed an attachment to the business park, creating an ongoing art project based on his many walks there, taking photos and making pictures. Marc grew up on the Isle of Man, the British Crown dependency in the Irish Sea, which he believed might be why he was drawn to this island of industrial premises, surrounded by marshland and the gigantic hulks of the Lenzing Fibers factory and Novartis Pharmaceuticals. They evoked his childhood view of the British landscape, which had nothing to do with rolling hills, chalk downs, mills and cricket pitches. 'As a kid on the Isle of Man, big old England was a shadowy entity on the horizon,' he says. 'On a clear day I could see the towers of Sellafield.' For the young Renshaw, England was a *Blade Runner* world of belching chimneys and towers, concrete stacks, smoke and flame. It was what he found attractive about the mainland, and why he was attracted to the same kind of vista as an adult.

Listening to Marc's memories, I was reminded of my own childhood relationship with a factory. In 1980 I lived next to large scrubby field alongside the electrified railway line that brought the local train into Glossop from Manchester. Beyond the low Victorian bridge that carried the railway line was a junk yard filled with broken machinery and corrugated iron. It was part of an industrial estate around the Ferro Alloys factory, from which a 400-foot white chimney loomed, like a rocket ready to launch. It had been built only three years earlier, but as far as I knew at the time, it had been there forever. I remember long summer Saturdays spent in its presence, out in the long grass, climbing trees and organising secret spy rings while hunkered down among tangles of hedgerows in dens we built from what we salvaged from the junk yard, until Dad called us home for tea. Northumbrian poet Paul Summers describes a similar childhood near the site of a factory in his poem 'In the Shadow of Chimneys', playing war on the no man's land of waste grounds, stalking rival neighbourhood kids while clutching penknives, and playing 'clammy sex games' among the elderberries.

The Ferro Alloys chimney is a consistent feature in my memories of that period. It is visible in the background of a photograph of me and my brother playing with a rugby ball,

The author (right) with Simon Rees in the
field beside the Ferro Alloys factory.

and in another of him hurtling towards the finish line on a
school sports day. It is even in a pile of old newspaper clippings
that I kept as a teen. Among articles about Bob Dylan, Sylvia
Plath and Roald Dahl is a cartoon drawn by Tony Husband,
dated 1989, entitled *Mr Clean (He's So Green)*. It depicts a
middle-aged, mummy's-boy superhero who comes to the res-
cue of a town named Blossop, where a tall chimney has been
belching poison. He blocks it with a boulder but after a few
hours the build-up of pressure blasts the rock skyward, and it
comes crashing down onto Mr Clean's kitchen table just as he
is asking his mother what's for dinner. 'Rock cakes,' she replies.

For me, the chimney was the icon of the town. A sign that I was home. You could use it to navigate to our house and it could be seen from miles away on the Snake Pass, the famously twisty road through the peaks that overlook the town. A black coil snaked its way around the upper half of the chimney, which led me to associate it with the pass, not only because of its serpentine shape but also because I knew that mythical snakes were seen as both seductive and deadly. After all, the Snake Pass was notorious for its high death toll, while the chimney – as illustrated in Tony Husband's cartoon – was accused of poisoning the townsfolk with toxins. There were days when a weird smell pervaded Glossop, a synthetic, cheesy stench of sulphur dioxide that was unbearable at times, and could not be escaped, even when we shut the doors and windows.

My brother and I were not allowed to cross beneath the railway line to the area around the factory. The bridge was our border. We loved to crouch in its darkness and feel the vibrations of the train running overhead. Whenever I heard that chugga-chug sound, I'd think about the dog that had been decapitated by a train's wheels one night after it ran away from its owner onto the line. I can't remember who told me the story but I have a vivid recollection of what the dog looked like in my imagination, a mongrel with wiry brown hair, truncated at the neck with only a red disc where it had been sliced. In my mind, as the train rumbled onward, the dog's head would roll over the other side of the track, down the embankment towards the factory, where it would come to rest in a puddle beside a discarded tyre, its glassy eyes reflecting the moon. I wonder, in retrospect, if my parents or the parents of one of my friends used the story as a cautionary tale to stop us from venturing too close to the line or the forbidden factory, to which we were nonetheless lured like Hansel and Gretel, drawn not by sweets but by the chunks of corrugated iron that made great bike ramps. Perhaps there never was a dead dog but, fictional or not, the image of it has stayed with me for forty years. Now, reanimated in these pages, maybe the headless dog of Glossop shall forever prowl that railway embankment, his severed neck howling at the moon.

Long after my family left the town, the factory closed, the fumes stopped, and the chimney was condemned, which upset those who wished it to be conserved. One idea was that it could be turned into a vertical garden. Another that a viewing platform could be installed at the top. Local artist Sean Wood suggested adding a fifty-foot statue of a hare to turn it into a landmark that might rival the Angel of the North, an interestingly folkloric choice, the hare being associated with magic and the otherworld. These ideas came to nothing and the chimney was dismantled in 2016. When I went to visit a few years later, the field where I played as a child was still there, and even a few of the trees I climbed. I could still crouch beneath the Victorian bridge with its dripping walls and continue through to where the junk yard used to be, except that it was now a gated trading estate with motor-repair centres, tool companies, medical-supply businesses and dog-groomers. But the Ferro

Alloys factory was gone and, without its chimney, there seemed to be a piece of my youth missing, a blank spot in my memory. A polluting carbuncle it might have been, but it represented where I lived, and my memories had entwined around it.

Industrial buildings are part of my heritage. My dad worked as a personnel manager at an alloy factory on the edge of town, which I'd visit in the school holidays so that we could go running together. My paternal grandfather, Brian Rees, was a floor supervisor at the Brymbo Steelworks in North Wales and my Uncle Vaughn a blacksmith there. My maternal grandfather, George Wright, was a salesman for Tennent's Lager, whose Glasgow brewery has nestled on the banks of the Molendinar Burn at the foot of the city's Necropolis since 1891. Because the burn was the original water source, percolating first though the cemetery before it reached the brewery, a story went around that this is what gave its lager its unique tang – rather than a beer with body, *you get bodies in your beer*.

When my grandfather retired in 1986, the brewery made a video to commemorate his decades of service, which I remember watching in fascination as a twelve-year-old boy. The film opens with him in a car, window open, cigar in his mouth, barrelling around the brewery to the sound of gunfire, like something out of *The Professionals*. 'He is a legend in his own lifetime,' says one of his work pals. At one point he is interviewed on the roof of the brewery, with the Necropolis visible behind him. I can't help but wonder if it was a carefully chosen shot; my grandfather was a Freemason and it was Freemasons who planned the cemetery, which is allegedly laid out as a giant Masonic symbol. The Necropolis is also a focal point of the ancient communication lines described in Harry Bell's *Glasgow's Secret Geometry: the City's Oldest Mystery*. Watching the video as a boy, it was just Papa standing on an industrial building, but when I see it now, there he stands atop one of Scotland's oldest ongoing businesses, with a Masonic city of the dead behind him, built on a confluence of ancient ley lines, humming with the energy of Stone Age moon cults, and I get the overwhelming sense that something else was going on.

But what then of my Welsh grandfather? He died of lung cancer in 1976, so I was never aware of the Brymbo Steelworks as a child and I had never paid a visit. If I was to reconstruct my family's industrial mythos, I needed to remedy this.

ıııııııııııııı

An ironworks was founded in Brymbo in 1796 by the industrialist, John 'Iron Mad' Wilkinson, who earned his moniker because he liked to surround himself with iron creations. He slept on an iron bed, worked at an iron desk, kept an iron coffin in his office and today his bones lie beneath an iron obelisk in Cumbria. Brymbo's steel production began in the 1880s and continued until its closure in 1990, when over a thousand workers were made redundant, including my Uncle Vaughn.

It was March when I drove north-west from Wrexham towards what remains of the steelworks: a gouge in a hill, lined with stone walls, supported by buttresses, its cavity filled with rusting skeletal frames, chimney stacks, defunct machinery and shipping containers. The site was protected by security fences and surrounded by large tracts of grassed-over rubble, cut through with new roads built in preparation for forthcoming developments. The names of the roads bear the legacy of the works, Blast Road and Phoenix Drive, the phoenix being the mythical bird that dies in flame and is reborn from the ashes, much as iron is smelted in a furnace then reborn as steel, or as the Brymbo Steelworks has been destroyed and awaits regeneration.

Set into the slope at the rear was John Wilkinson's eighteenth-century blast furnace, vegetation pushing between the bricks, looking like the ruin of a Mayan temple. In front of it, a small steam locomotive rested on a narrow-gauge track. The machine-shop building to the left side of the works was roofless, its windows smashed. A row of blue plastic wheelie bins alongside a waterlogged ditch looked incongruous against the brown Victorian walls. Isolated in the foreground was the cylindrical smelting crucible, encrusted with ore, like the decapitated head of Ted Hughes's 'Iron Man' waiting for its body to return and pick it up. The place was silent but for the caw of crows circling in the sky. It felt like the aftermath of a catastrophe.

In 2017, the Fourth Element Paranormal Research group held a ghost hunt in the derelict works, a recording of which they published on YouTube. In the video, the group forms a circle and prays for protection before probing the interiors as dusk descends. Inside the machine shop they bang on a girder and listen for a response. They hold a seance, asking any spirits present to flicker the light as a sign. 'Come and touch me,' a medium says. 'Knock the hat off my head . . . pinch one of the ladies.' Nothing happens but some attendees claim that the room grows colder. Another medium claims that there is the ghost of a thirty-eight-year-old man in the room. 'Did you work here?' she asks. 'Did you die on this site?' The lack of answers to these questions doesn't put them off.

I wonder what my grandfather would have made of his workplace as a heritage ruin, infested with ghost hunters. Perhaps it was his spirit that lurked in the machine shop, but given what I know about his reputation, he wouldn't have needed a second invitation to give the ladies a cheeky pinch. At the age of twenty he was a Spitfire pilot in the Battle of Britain who watched most of his squadron perish in flames. He never got used to the pace of ordinary life after the war and developed a taste for gambling and womanising, as revealed to me in gory detail by my late grandmother one night after we had both put away too much gin and tonic. She loved him, but she was angry, very angry, even twenty-five years after his death. I've seen only a meagre handful of photos of him – a bald man with a handlebar moustache. Standing in the shattered steelworks, I tried to conjure up an image of Brian Rees in my mind, to picture the apparition of a man I never knew in a place that was no more.

In a melancholy mood, I returned to my car and drove up the hill to the back of the steelworks, where I parked outside a locked gate. A path ran alongside the works, lined with a lichen-green fence, curled with creepers. Through the slates I could see rail tracks and miniature trains, some of which seemed to have been used recently. At the end of a path, a stile crossed me into a field and up a slope to a rickety wooden gate bearing the faded words: BRYMBO STEELWORKS PROPERTY. A nearby telegraph pole was wrapped with a banner that read DRAIN EARTH, which felt appropriate in this exploited landscape. I followed the telegraph poles past piles of wood chippings to a wire fence with a human-sized hole cut into it. On the other side was a plateau of severed tree stumps and piled sticks, strewn with carrier bags, bottles and beer cans.

At the edge of the field I stood at the top of a steep slope, looking out. Down to my left lay the ruined works and to the right rolled undulating hills with electricity pylons marching out from a substation nestled within folds of green. From the distance came an agonised howl. I couldn't make out whether it was human or animal. Moments later I spotted two massive black dogs trotting down the opposite slope to mine. There was no owner in sight. These dogs were on their own, moving with purpose in a steady trot. They did not stop to play or sniff, remaining resolutely one behind the other. It was surprising how much ground they covered, and how swiftly. Soon they reached the bottom of the hill, and started to ascend towards me. I grew nervous. I love dogs but not these dogs. These dogs were up to something, if they were even dogs at all. Being no longer certain, I decided to return to the car.

I later discovered that since the 1920s there have been sightings in Brymbo of the Gwyllgi, a Black Dog in Welsh folk-lore – variously described as cow-sized with shaggy pelts and wide faces. Apparently there was a particular flurry of Gwyllgi sightings here in the 1970s during the final heydays of the foundry, and the last years of my grandfather's life. As Brian Rees strolled between clanging machinery with his clipboard in hand, was he too stalked by these legendary beasts, lurking on this hill, flames reflected in their hungry eyes?

⁗⁗⁗⁗⁗⁗⁗⁗⁗

There appears to be something about steelworks in Wales that seeps into the imagination and folklore of the local population. On the south coast, Port Talbot is a steel town clinging onto its industry against all the economic odds. Perhaps it owes its survival to an eight-hundred-year-old wall in the grounds of the works owned by Tata Steel. The story goes that in the sixteenth century a Cistercian monk cursed the remains of a farmhouse, of which the wall formed one side. This hex was revenge for Henry VIII's dissolution of the monasteries, which had finished off the monk's order, forcing him to leave the nearby abbey. As a parting shot he decreed that should the wall ever fall, the whole of Port Talbot would fall with it. In recent years there have been sightings of a phantom monk prowling the grounds, keeping an eye on his wall, which remains intact thanks to maintenance by the steelworks' owners, keen perhaps not to ruin the town's fortunes.

105

It is not the only structure in the Tata Steel works that has a morbid story to tell. There is also a sculpture of a pickaxe, forging tool and shovel, made to commemorate an explosion in the pit in 1890, which killed 178 workers. The day after, rescuers spotted a hand sticking through a gap in the blocks of coal. It belonged to a boy named Oates, who had been employed to carry buckets of grease, and who was miraculously still alive. As he emerged into the light, he is said to have declared, 'Oh, my, what a lot of rubbish we have got through.' He was one of the lucky ones; it is believed that the bodies of at least fifteen of the men were never recovered and that they lie entombed two hundred metres below the works. It remains a dangerous business to this day; a series of explosions on a train carrying molten metal through the factory shook the town in April 2019. In Port Talbot, where so many people have worked in the same industry for generations, the past is never far away, and can still rattle the nerves of the populace.

In this way, factories can often cast a malevolent influence over the towns in which they are situated, emanating rumbles and noises that seep into the dreams of sleepers. For two years in Swansea, a ghostly siren would wake people up before the crack of dawn and persist through the early morning. A resident named Debbie Leyshon told the local press that it was 'just like a siren you hear in the war films'. Swansea was intensely bombed during the Second World War as the Luftwaffe attempted to hobble the nation's coal supply in a three-day blitz. Newspapers speculated that the ghostly dawn siren was some kind of echo of that deadly event, the contemporary city haunted by its collective wartime memories. The disturbance was serious enough for officials to embark on an investigation of the ghostly wails, with no success for a year, until the source was finally detected. It turned out to be the siren used as part of the emergency evacuation drill at Vale Europe nickel refinery in Clydach, some six miles north-east of the city centre.

Some factories enter local lore in more subtle ways, especially when they are shrouded in mystery and rumour. In 1966, Bobby Seal, an eleven-year-old boy from Mold, went walking with his friends in the Rhydymwyn Valley in Flintshire, North Wales. Usually they'd stop by the river to try to catch fish with their bare hands, but on this day, they felt adventurous and followed the river upstream into unfamiliar territory. Sunlight flickered through gaps in the treetop canopy as the boys pushed further up the valley, which began to narrow and darken as its sides rose ever more steeply. Bobby tells the story:

> The grass underfoot was lush and untrodden, suggesting that few others ever walked this way. We all felt uneasy, though none of us would admit it. We laughed and joked, trying to lighten the oppressive mood, but soon we fell silent. Even the birds ceased their singing. As we rounded a bend in the river, we beheld the massive rampart of what appeared to be an ancient fortress: a high concrete wall spanning the narrow neck of the valley, crested with metal railings and barbed wire. We edged closer, wary of our

proximity to the river, which was now a narrow channel, dark and foreboding. However, the path came to an end and we were unable to proceed any further. Not wishing to linger in this gloomy spot, we retraced our steps and re-emerged into the world of light.

Several days later I told my dad about our walk and asked him if he knew anything about the strange dam up the valley. He told me that we'd clearly walked a long way and that the dam was part of the perimeter of an old factory. The factory was dangerous, he told me, and we should keep well clear of it.

My friends and I did keep away. But that wasn't quite the end of it. Throughout my childhood I picked up snippets of talk from adult conversations referencing the 'bomb factory'. Was it a real place or just part of local folklore?

Bobby discovered as an adult that during the Second World War ICI ran a chemical weapons research facility known first as the X-Site and then the Valley Works. It was one of a series of secret and carefully protected factories used to manufacture and store mustard gas, despite its use being banned under the Geneva Protocol. The Rhydymwyn Valley was ideal for such a facility because of its steep sides and dense woodland, which concealed the factory from enemy bombers, and its natural limestone tunnels, which could be used to keep the chemicals safe. Bobby also told me: 'The factory was involved in some of the early gas diffusion experiments that formed the basis for the Manhattan Project – the Allied nuclear bomb. Later it played an important role in experiments which led to the development of the first British nuclear weapon.'

Because of the extreme sensitivity of its operations, the factory's existence was kept hush-hush, existing only in fragments of adult chatter that Bobby heard as a youngster. There was much speculation about how else the valley's limestone tunnels were used after the war, but the only confirmed function was to house strategic food stores during the 1950s and 1960s for use in national emergency. Even today, says Bobby, officials are cagey about allowing access to the now derelict site, which is fenced off and patrolled by guards. Sentry boxes line the old rails that used to carry materials between its various flat-roofed buildings, spaced out so that if one exploded, there would not be a chain reaction. These were now empty. Their loading platforms overgrown. Paintwork peeling. Flanked by signs reading:'DANGER: Keep Out'. Derelict or not, it seemed there were still things inside this place that needed to be kept out of the public eye.

In 2015 Bobby gained permission to explore the bomb factory, so long as he was accompanied by a guide. As he reached the southern end of the site, the valley began to close in on him. The light dimmed and it grew cold, evoking a sensation that he'd not felt since his boyhood adventure in 1966. At a corner of fencing, he looked through the slats to see a steep drop to the valley below. He was standing on the top of a concrete dam: the same fortress in the woods that he had gazed up at as an eleven-year-old. Water trickled down the wall and pooled in a

narrow channel far below. And there, at the foot of the structure that had haunted his memories for almost half a century,
he thought he could see four young boys gawping up at him,
silent and wide-eyed.

||||||||||||||||

I pass all my hours in a tumbledown field,
Rememb'ring the happiness to me she did yield
I survey ev'ry walk now my chimney is gone,
And sigh when I think that I'm now all alone;
O then 'tis, O then that I think there's no Hell
Like loving too well

But the whiffs of sulphuric egg reminds me
Of how life used to feel by the old factory
As I look to the sky where her smoke left a stain,
I imagine those thrills may yet come again;
O then 'tis, O then that no joy's above
The pleasures of love

But when I consider the truth of her part
In the poison and violence she once did impart
I do fear I she has wrong'd us and so she may be
An evil that lingers in my memory
O then 'tis, O then I think no fear is above
The terror of love

5

INTO THE
UNDERWORLD

THE CULT OF FLYOVERS
AND UNDERPASSES

The doll on the bridge above Bristol's M32 took us by surprise. She was made of hard plastic, dressed in a black-and-white embroidered frock. Possibly vintage, but it seemed wrong to pull up her dress to check for markings, so carefully had she been positioned. She sat upright against a graffitied metal fence, legs stuck out in front of her. One of her shoes had lost its sole. Her eyes looked down and to the left in melancholic contemplation. Some of her blond hair tumbled over her shoulders, but the rest was tied in a ponytail, entwined with a strut in the fence above her, a twig fixing it in place. She clutched a bunch of yellow roses, one arm clamped over the stems and the other resting on the withered heads. A few purple tulip heads protruded from her lap. There was no card or note to explain her presence.

'Why is that thing here?' I asked my companions, Nick and Mark, who both live in this city, but they didn't know. Directly below, motorway traffic flowed down a river of tarmac while vehicles rose and fell on the slip roads to either side, before whirling around us on the elevated roundabout. We stared in silence, as if the answer would somehow emanate from the doll if we waited long enough. Perhaps she was a shrine in memory of someone who jumped into the traffic, or a murder victim. Perhaps this doll had nothing to do with death, but with life;

an effigy of a child holding flowers might be a votive offering to nature. Or perhaps this was nothing more than a spontaneous act by a passer-by who simply picked up a discarded doll and placed it there to be found, or to confound. Whatever the reason, she made me think about this spot in which she had been placed: a motorway interchange formed of underpasses, overpasses and elevated roads. There was something about her – some hint of reverence and ritual – that suggested Junction 3 of the M32 might have a meaning for some people that stretches beyond its basic functionality.

Before we discovered the doll, the three of us had set out on foot from Mark's flat in St Paul's, central Bristol, on a gloriously sunny Saturday in early February, with no other aim than to amble, talk and see what we could find. The streets were alive with people emerging from the darkness of winter. Parks bustled with families. Shrieks of children filled the air. The street art on the walls was vibrant with colour in the sunshine. As we drifted through Ashley Street park, towards the M32, Mark described some of the characters who lived in these streets, such as the man whose home used to be concealed behind a stack of refrigerators piled as high as the roof, known as 'Fridge-henge', before the property was demolished to make way for flats. He pointed my gaze towards a large Victorian house, once home to a graphic designer and journalist named Angie. 'A New Age type,' said Mark. 'She bought the house to use as a women's refuge but lived there alone for twenty years. The top floor was derelict, with a tree growing through one of its back rooms. Pigeons lived on the tree inside the house with her.'

On the approach to Junction 3, the pavement veered us away from the road and onto a footpath alongside a smooth convex wall that curved gracefully around the exterior of the roundabout, every inch covered in graffiti: BUGGER BREXIT in Union Jack letters; a skull wearing a snake as a bandana; a rabbit with a spliff-shaped carrot in his mouth asking:'WHAT'S UP DOC?'

'Years ago, it was risky to walk around these parts,' said Mark as we approached the underpass entrance, covered in a collage of fly posters and stickers, scuffed and torn, bearing fragments of band names, the faces of stern-looking DJs and dates of techno parties. We passed through the dark tunnel, where lurid painted characters on the walls leered in the half-light, and emerged into the interior of the interchange, a park of unkempt grass and pine trees, traversed by footpaths, resplendent with early-season daffodils. Before us was a black rectangular steel object: a makeshift shrine with a rusty brown bowl bolted onto its frontage, containing what seemed to be offerings of dried fruits, seeds and petals. A purple ribbon was tied to one side and a boot lace to the other.

In its top-left corner was a symbol consisting of two triangles inside a white circle, their apexes meeting in the centre. It was most probably meant to be the logo for the environmental movement Extinction Rebellion, which explains: 'The circle signifies the planet, while the hourglass inside serves as

The shrine.

a warning that time is rapidly running out for many species.' It felt pertinent that this symbol of climate resistance had been etched onto a shrine within a motorway interchange, a conduit for carbon monoxide that exists only because of the combustion engine, one of the contributing factors to global warming. Positioned less than a hundred metres away from the doll on the bridge, it seemed to represent an interaction of some kind with the structure in which it was placed. Whether it was a challenge to the very existence of the motorway, or an attempt to mitigate its effects with an offering to nature, I did not know. But I do know that this is a place with a dark past.

Between 1966 and 1975 the M32 bulldozed its way through historical areas of central Bristol such as St Paul's, St Agnes, Baptist Mills and Easton. A BBC report described the motorway as a 'dagger thrust into the heart of the city'. Communities were split in two. Former neighbours now lived on opposite sides of a treacherous river of traffic. For those inhabitants of Victorian terraces in the path of the motorway, it was a case of obliteration via compulsory purchase order. Residents were relocated to distant suburbs such as Southmead and Hartcliffe. St Agnes stopped existing as an area in everything but name. Lower Ashley Road, a busy thoroughfare running through St Paul's, was bifurcated by the Junction 3 interchange: underpasses allowing pedestrians to move beneath the roundabout and a bridge to take them over the motorway. With Lower Ashley Road split, businesses withered on either side and the area suffered from a lack of local education services, poor housing conditions and rising racial tensions. In 1980, police suspected drug dealing inside the Black and White Café on Grosvenor Road and stormed the building. Violence erupted and a full-scale riot spread down the road towards the motorway junction. In the decades that followed, turf wars raged between drug gangs in St Paul's and violent crime soared. The underpasses of the junction were not a place to stroll if you didn't have your wits about you. Many locals would catch a bus into the city centre to avoid walking through them.

Since then its paths have become worn with the feet of hundreds of thousands of people. Passing decades have chipped away at its veneer. Traces of spilled blood have entered its DNA. The underpass walls are infused with ganja smoke. Lovers have screwed in the bushes. Deals have been done. Lives have ended. Art has coated almost every available surface. Fences have been tagged. Flowers have grown. Trees have seeded. Rampant gentrification in the centre of Bristol has spread outward from areas like Montpelier and Stokes Croft into the areas surrounding the junction, gradually softening its hard reputation. It is now a popular and relatively safe thoroughfare with the atmosphere of an urban park; an oasis of greenery in which to dwell.

'I drive down this bit of motorway almost every day,' mused Nick, 'but I cannot remember the last time I walked up here. I should do it more often.'

One of the striking qualities of a motorway interchange is that it appears very different in design, function and cultural meaning, depending on your position and mode of transit through it. A driver on the M32 can see only the exit ramp and a concrete bridge pass overhead, gone in the blink of an eye. The parkland and painted underpasses are part of an invisible world they might never even know about, and might as well not exist, despite them passing within metres of it. For a driver who exits at the junction and whirls around the gyratory, the interior is glimpsed only briefly as a burst of foliage through a gap in the fence.

However, pedestrians experience the structure in a totally different way. Over many minutes, even hours, they negotiate curved walls and rectangular passageways covered in art, tags, political messages and advertising. They can smell car fumes, cigarette smoke and cut grass, touch the surfaces, leave their offerings, linger in the shade, hang out with some mates. A pedestrian might remember a time in the 1960s before the interchange existed; those battles with the police that raged on the nearby roads in the 1980s; that time they bought or sold some weed in the underpasses; or how this was once a route to a lover's house, or that of a friend now gone. These memories might evoke complex emotions, take them back in time to lost states. A space like this can therefore be many, often contradictory, things at once: ugly and beautiful; loved and disregarded; remembered and forgotten. Even beyond a purely anthropocentric viewpoint, the interchange is an object with its own story, more complex than that of any single human individual who uses it, threading together multiple functions, cultures and histories. As the philosopher Graham Harman says, 'Landscape is any object that links a wide variety of other objects that all use it as a mediator. A landscape is like a "wormhole" linking different times and different places of living organisms and inanimate objects.'[20] This thrumming nexus of concrete, vegetation, humans and machines feels like the epitome of that idea.

As we walked the junction's circuit of paths we passed cyclists and joggers, lovers walking hand in hand and folk milling about on the grass. For some people this is a place to dream, play and get high. On the back of an information sign, sprayed in psychedelic pinks and yellows, were drawn a dozen magic mushrooms and the words LIBERTY CAPS. A red fly agaric mushroom was painted on the back of a metal electrical enclosure. The words PLAY NICE were daubed on a metal fence. In this overtly non-natural structure a rich spiritual life appeared to be flourishing, inspiring the devotional shrine full of offerings and the doll with the roses. Something about the circular structure and intersecting causeways of the junction reminded me of ancient ceremonial sites such as Arbor Low Stone Circle in the Peak District or Newgrange, a passage tomb in County Meath, in which a stone circle surrounds a mound ringed with white quartz, where votive offerings have been found. And then there is Huly Hill Cairn to the west of Edinburgh, where the automotive age literally overlays the Bronze Age; an interchange of the M9 motorway ringing a large ancient burial mound among fragments of what was once a stone circle. I wondered what archaeologists will make of the ruins of Bristol's Junction 3 in seven thousand years' time. Possibly their conjectures will resemble those of our present-day experts ruminating over prehistoric remnants.

'People would travel down great tarmac causeways to congregate in the interior of this circular ceremonial structure,' they might explain, 'where they left offerings to nature, daubed art on the walls and carried out rituals. But for what purpose? Blood sacrifices? Solstice celebrations? Shamanic drug trips? The coronation of kings and queens? We shall never know. All we can say is that the people of twenty-first-century Bristol were deeply attuned to the landscape and to the seasons. A time which, sadly, has been lost.'

॥॥॥॥॥॥॥॥॥॥

On a second trip the next day, alone this time, I took a walk a little further north to the Eastville Flyover at Junction 2 of the M32. Instead of cutting through the city, here the motorway soared above the trees and houses, then swooped down across the front of a 1930s terrace, before swinging out over Tesco and IKEA, towards the city centre. To take traffic down to the ground, access roads split from either side of the elevated motorway and fell in graceful angles towards the roundabout interchange below. The flyover seemed monstrously out of proportion to the houses; an invader from a world of giants paying no regard to the Lilliputian civilisation that lies beneath it.

Amid the whiff of petroleum and the grinding gears of ascending trucks I could feel the pavement vibrate as I used a subway to cross under the roundabout and emerge into its central island of pathways, street lamps and lawns. It felt as if I was standing in a cathedral, thick columns holding up the vast concrete canopy of the M32 above, shafts of holy light beaming through the gaps created where one slip road separated from another.

As I had discovered in neighbouring Junction 3 there was an abundance of artworks, all of which seemed to be about the connection – or disconnection – between the urban and natural. On one pillar a child held onto a dandelion clock that carried her up towards the motorway, shedding seed spores in the shape of musical notes. On another, a fish swam in a choppy river while dragonflies passed above. Then on the side of a low ledge was painted the silhouette of a city skyline, resplendent with chimney stacks, tower blocks and church spires, viewed as though through newly parted fronds of long jungle grass, like a vision of the future glimpsed from a deep rural past. There was political art too: Extinction Rebellion signs; anti-police slogans; and the phrase 'Solidarity with *die drei von der park bank*' ('the three from the park bench') – a reference to the arrest in 2019 of anti-capitalist activists in Hamburg allegedly preparing an arson attack on the anniversary of the G20 riots.

A thin man with dreadlocks carefully counted the bottles of water he had stacked inside a shopping trolley. His tent was pitched in front of the railings among piles of bric-a-brac and cardboard boxes of all sizes. He carefully took off his dirty top and exchanged it for another dirty top, then he looked out at the traffic, as if watching for something. With the shelter that it provides from rain, this was a natural refuge for the homeless, notorious as a zone of drug deals, sexual congress and improvised camping. In the entrance of a urine-streaked underpass, a figure shifted inside a sleeping bag. On the ground outside was an embossed metal compass star. I took the northerly direction, walking the length of the flyover, past a woman sitting on a pallet while a man photographed her, and two abandoned cars with smashed windows and wheel-clamps, until I came to the River Frome, a narrow weed-straggled waterway flowing beneath the stone bridge. On the other side of the water was a barn with wooden doors, signposted 'Bridge Farm'. It was an odd scene to encounter beneath the concrete ceiling of the flyover, as if people in a rural village had woken up one morning to find a hard sky above, rumbling with the thunder of unseen gods, their world cast into an eternal gloom. As I took some photos, a well-dressed woman came up to me with a bundle of groceries in her arms and tears in her eyes.

'Can you help me?' she said in an Eastern European accent. 'I'm lost! My phone is in the pram with my mother. I went to Tesco but now I cannot find them. I only moved here a day ago. I don't know where I live.'

I asked for the number and called it, handing the phone to her. She listened as it rang, and rang, until the answerphone message kicked in.

'They won't hear it,' she said, sadly. 'It's in the pram.'

'We should keep trying,' I said, redialling and listening as the phone rang out again. The traffic was so noisy it was hard to hear the answerphone message. We made a few more attempts before I advised her to wait in Tesco, as her mother would surely return there to find her, and it was only at the other end of the flyover. She wiped away a tear, as if resolved to follow the plan, but she seemed unsure and didn't follow when I suggested we walk in the direction of the supermarket. Perhaps her mother would never appear and she would be doomed to live forever beneath the flyover. Perhaps she had *always* been here, going in loops, like the traffic on the interchange, trapped in a vortex of whirling machines.

In J. G. Ballard's novel *Concrete Island*, published in 1974, a man's car runs off a motorway interchange and crashes into an area of waste ground penned off on all sides by steep embankments. Injured and seemingly alone on this island amid its 'labyrinth of ascent ramps and feeder lanes', the protagonist Maitland becomes a contemporary Robinson Crusoe, 'alone on an alien planet abandoned by its inhabitants, a race of motorway builders who had long since vanished but had bequeathed to him this concrete wilderness'.[21] In the wasteland Maitland finds traces of Edwardian house foundations, a cinema, printing shop, air-raid shelter and churchyard – ruins sealed off by the construction of the motorway interchange and left to decay. He soon discovers that there are others on the island: a woman named Jane Shephard and a brain-damaged tramp called Proctor. As the wounded Maitland struggles to escape, he enters into a complex relationship with his two companions, and gradually any sense of his life before the accident begins to recede as he readjusts to life in the motorway wilderness, until the reader begins to suspect he has no intention of leaving the place at all.

Here too, beneath the M32, it was all too easy for me to imagine its inhabitants as voluntarily trapped. A woman perpetually searching for her mother. A man endlessly count-ing his bottles of water. A sleeper on a piss-soaked floor. People for whom this island was both a sanctuary and a hell.

That is not to say, however, that a flyover must always be a pariah. Sometimes they can be loved. In 1967, a temporary prefabricated flyover was erected behind Bristol's Temple Meads station in order to reduce congestion. It contained a single lane for cars, connecting Temple Way with Redcliffe Way in one direction only. Held aloft on spindly struts, with metal barriers on either side, it looked more like a rollercoaster than a con-duit for traffic, taking cars steeply up in a rightward curve then dipping back to the ground again shortly afterwards. When it opened, it was decried as an eyesore. Traffic engineers warned that motorists would feel 'a certain strangeness'[22] when they used it.

Despite this, the Redcliffe Flyover became embraced as a quirky anomaly of the city – a welcome part of the city's culture. It even has somewhat of a supporting role in Christopher Petit's 1979 cult British road movie *Radio On*, in which the protagonist, Robert, drives from London to Bristol to investigate his broth-er's death in a Britain teetering on the brink of the Thatcher era. Robert's arrival in Bristol is heralded by the Redcliffe Flyover, sodium lights reflected in the puddles on its dimpled tarmac. It is seen again as he parks up at the Grosvenor Hotel, framed so that it is as dominant in the shot as the hotel, an unusual perspective at the time, when such structures would often have been edited out. In an interview with Adam Scovell for the BFI in 2019 Petit discusses why he hired the film's German cameraman Martin Schäfer: 'I showed him a field with a pylon in it and asked how he would frame the shot.' With the pylon in the middle of the frame,' he said, and I knew I could trust him to see what I saw, only better.' Likewise, the Redcliffe Flyover is a marginal structure given centrality, not only to the visual aesthetic, but to the story itself. In almost every shot of a city road during *Radio On* there is a flyover, as if it is carrying not only cars, but the narrative of the film. In one scene, as Robert stands in his hotel room talking to his German companions, the Redcliffe Flyover becomes the conduit for a nocturnal tracking shot, taken from a car ascending its rickety spine, catching the protagonists in the glow of the window in the adjacent Grosvenor Hotel, before descending again into the inky monochrome gloom.

In 1998, after thirty-one years of service, the flyover was pulled down and replaced with a roundabout. While some Bristolians were relieved, the reaction from most was sadness. Some fans even drove to the city with the sole purpose of using the flyover once more before it was demolished. Footage was posted on YouTube and photographs on Flickr attracting comments such as:

'We were always going over the Flyover, it was the closest thing we got to flying in the 1970s.'

'Sadly missed.'

'It was like you were taking off. Great memories.'

'It should never have been taken down. It was a monument of Bristol.'

Like the Eiffel Tower, built as a temporary structure never intended to be an enduring Parisian landmark, the Redcliffe Flyover became totemic. It came to represent fun, thrills and amusement; rare moments of child-like wonder in the midst of a tough, troubled city. A similar process of appropriation can happen to other unlikely landmarks such as chimneys, communications masts and factories. As we grow up among them they become ingrained within our memories and shared history. What can seem at first ugly and soulless can gradually come to accumulate emotional resonance through the sheer power of persistence.

Take the UK's most famous flyover, the Gravelly Hill Interchange, otherwise known as Spaghetti Junction, in Birmingham. This confluence of motorways and A-roads has been elevated to a kind of mythic status. People know about it even if they have never driven on it or walked beneath it. Its name is used colloquially as shorthand for the ugly insanity of modern life, representing the damage wrought in the twentieth century by our need for speed and convenience, which has resulted in the pervasive roadscapes that now scar the country. At Spaghetti Junction there are flyovers flying over flyovers, carrying two hundred thousand vehicles every day on five levels of road. There are many aerial photos of this infamously mad tangle but what is less known is that there is an inhabited place below.

Beneath the tumult of machines, anglers sit on riverbanks, ducks paddle on rippled waters, insects buzz between flowers and joggers puff beneath the concrete columns. Along the canalside is a mural of a tropical jungle scene, the green fronds reflected in the water, a portal to a deeper past. *The Lost Tales* podcast describes how this hidden world contains 'old paths buried under giant serpents of concrete and tarmac' and 'a river forgotten underneath the madness of the modern world'. In his film *Living Under Spaghetti** Joe Sampson talks to some of the people who live their lives beneath the junction, interviewing a narrow-boater who describes pockets of peace and quiet where time seems to slow. Another local describes what is 'up there' – the concrete knot in the sky – as 'madness' while what is below is 'reality'. Far from being an unwelcome by-product of the junction, these people feel that their subterranean world is the truly valid space, invisible as it may be to most. They're like the Borrowers in Mary Norton's novel of the same name: tiny occupants of a structure that they share with giants who barely register their existence. The interviewees seem to be more than content that theirs is a disregarded paradise – a secret that they can keep to themselves. They are the happy alternative to Ballard's bleak vision in *Concrete Island*, showing that humans can find contentment beneath the maligned roadscapes of the late twentieth century.

---

* Part of his film series, *Lost But Not Forgotten.*

In 2014, the artist Bill Drummond began to create art beneath Spaghetti Junction, based around performance, graffiti and photography. In one piece he floated along a waterway on a raft made from his bed, filled with bunches of daffodils in four hundred jam jars. His passion for the junction was inspired by an incident in his teenage years when he was hitchhiking down the M6 in 1973. Dropped off beneath Spaghetti Junction, he tried to find his way out but ended up walking through what he described as its 'labyrinth' for hours as the sun went down. As he watched a narrowboat pass by on the canal, he felt as if he had journeyed into a lost age, and decided to sleep on the towpath that night, where he dreamed that beneath Spaghetti Junction lay the entrance to the Underworld.

This association between a motorway and a gateway to another world is made by the poet and author Salena Godden in her memoir *Springfield Road*. As an infant she lived in Danesholme in Corby, Northamptonshire, where she would play a game with her best friend that involved spying on her older brother and his friends near the motorway underpass at the fringe of their housing estate.

> We followed them through the tunnel that led under the motorway and towards the woods on the edge of the estate. We weren't allowed to go there. It was dark and cool beneath the underpass, with the steady roar of traffic above us, we made a racket, roaring and shouting as we ran through the dark and the urine stench towards the sunlight. We believed that there were real grizzly bears in

Danesholme woods, so we didn't follow my brother any further at first. We stayed safe in the sunshine, peering at the edge where the trees started, before the long forest shadows began.[23]

For the little girl finding her way in the world, the underpass in Corby was a border crossing between the sanctuary of the housing estate and a wild, untamed country where mythic grizzly bears might rule, not humans.

The underpasses and flyovers found at these urban perimeters become places where youngsters go to hide from adults so that they can play, drink, smoke and express themselves away from those who mock the way they dress and the music to which they listen. In their dark recesses, teenage goths, punks, ravers, metalheads and grime headz, who have no other place to go can create their own clubs and boozers. Turner Prize-winning artist Mark Leckey used to hang out as a child beneath a M53 motorway bridge near his home in Birkenhead, Wirral. He claims that when he was nine years old, a 'pixie, fairy, elf creature' appeared to him under the motorway. It was an event he accepted as fact until his late teens when rationality began to chip away at his memory. However, his vision beneath the motorway was formative. At the end of his 1999 video work *Fiorucci Made Me Hardcore*, in which he uses found footage of UK dance scenes from the 1960s to the 1990s, he includes looped footage of a dancing figure. Leckey explained that 'in folklore the fairies would entrance people into a never-ending dance, a wild delirium that wouldn't stop'[24] just as the hedonism of the rave scene could lure working-class teenagers into its perpetual cycle of weekend parties.

He pushed this idea even further in his 2019 Tate Britain installation *O' Magic Power of Bleakness* which recreated the space beneath his childhood flyover in a life-size replica, and included an audio-visual drama about five teenage friends who hang out there, depicted as black-and-white projections, huddled in the alcove. 'Is this bridge from one hundred years ago or, like, from one thousand years ago?' says one of them as the camera tracks downward, beneath ground level, descending through subterranean megalithic stone chambers. Just as I saw hints of Neolithic ritualist geometries in Junction 3 of the M32, Leckey's film makes links between the structure of the M53 flyover and prehistory. Despite the overlay of super-modernity, the folkloric past persists and the flyover has become a conduit for new spells. In fragmented audio clips the boys josh with each other and one shouts, 'You're away with the fairies, Mark!' But their jocularity sours as odd smells and noises spook them in the gloom. It turns out that these twenty-first-century teenagers are being stalked beneath the concrete by spiteful supernatural entities. Eventually, one of the boys is stolen by fairies and replaced with a changeling as the group becomes entranced by pounding tribal music, contorting their bodies into flyover-like shapes.

Leckey's work is an example of the complex relationship we have with the intersections of motorways in our communities.

They harbour an alternative culture, offering sanctuary and joy for the young and disaffected, but they also divide communities and destroy landscapes. In 1966, a new section of the M4 was built in the steel town of Port Talbot, South Wales, to allow the motorway to move seamlessly between Swansea and Cardiff, cutting twenty minutes off the journey. There was very little space to put the motorway, as the mountains were so close to the sea, so they built it on 45-foot-high pillars at the rear of the town at a cost of £5 million. But it came at a social cost too, requiring the demolition of three chapels and hundreds of houses. An article in the *Western Mail* said that the consolation for all these troubles would be that this futuristic sky-borne roadway could become one of the great sights of Wales. It was a deal with the devil, the results of which had to be reckoned with by those whose homes remained standing. The shape of their world was irrevocably altered as great white pillars loomed over their street, concrete walls replaced the houses of their neighbours opposite, combustion engines coughed above their roofs and the hiss of tyres became their dawn chorus. They received no compensation for their troubles. Their suffering, as far as the planners were concerned, was simply a necessary sacrifice to the gods of economic progress, in exchange for the benefits of having this new high-speed corridor between London and Wales.

In recent years, the historian Dr Martin Johnes has argued that the planners were right, claiming that the M4 in South Wales is 'the most important place in Welsh history' and that the country would be unimaginable without it and its power to establish a sense of place in those who used it. 'To travel down the M4 is to see South Wales,' he writes. 'Everything from castles to country houses and steelworks to government office blocks.'[25]

And, of course, for those children who grew up after its construction, there was nothing controversial about it; the M4 flyover was as inherent to the local landscape as the mountains behind the town, or the billowing chimneys on the skyline. Resident Paul Phillips recalls his 1970s childhood beneath the motorway:

> As far as we were concerned, we had what was pretty much our own personal undercover tarmac play area that had a clear run of a good few hundred metres to race our Choppers along. Every bonfire night my dad would put a fire together. Typically, it would be raining but his stash of wood that he wombled and kept dry under the M4 could quickly be assembled and topped off with the Guy made out of last year's British Rail uniform. Plumes of smoke and rockets would go up over the motorway, reducing visibility to zero. We'd throw potatoes in the embers then eat them in our den of the day, back under the shelter of the M4. It was a weird childhood but I never knew any different. Once I grew up, I realised it was a brutal environment but at that point the M4 became my escape route. I'd stand on the slip road by the cemetery with my bass guitar, thumb out, and hitch a lift to London to play in a band.

For Paul the flyover was the theatre in which he played out his youth, bound up with the folk tradition of bonfires and memories of his father. The slip road he mentions comes down off the M4 and over St Mary's Churchyard, where lies the body of one Richard Lewis, otherwise known as Dic Penderyn, who in 1831 was hanged after allegedly stabbing a soldier during a riot in Merthyr Tydfil. At the time, Merthyr Tydfil was the centre of the global iron-making industry, but the workers had become discontented over their poor wages and the restrictions on their right to vote. Seeking reform, they marched through the streets of the town, raided the local debtors' court, reclaimed confiscated property and destroyed debtors' records. Growing nervous, their bosses called in the army and violence broke out, during which a soldier received stab wounds in his back. Despite there being no evidence that Dic Penderyn had committed the act, he was sentenced to death by hanging – a stark warning that any uprising that threatened the country's status as an economic powerhouse would be severely punished. To this day, his gravestone remains a popular tourist draw under the shadow of the flyover's slip road.

But another unofficial gravestone, of sorts, can be found elsewhere in those shadows: a tiled plinth, chest height, erected in memory of one of the streets of homes destroyed to make way for it. On one side it bears an OS map image of a Victorian terrace, rendered as an abstract purple block. On the other, a map of the original street, its demolished houses delineated beneath the dark smear of the flyover. The monument speaks volumes about the sense of loss that resulted from the motorway. In an echo of Dic Penderyn's story, people in Port Talbot

Memorial to a Lost Street, Port Talbot.

were expected to accept the destruction of their homes as a sacrifice in the name of economic growth.

Death seems to go hand in hand with this section of the Port Talbot Flyover. On one side of the slip road lies St Mary's Church and Dic Penderyn's grave, and on the other is the cemetery beside which Paul Phillips used to wait with his bass guitar for a ride. This cemetery shares one of its flanking walls with that of the road, its new brickwork so sympathetic to the original stone that the two entities have merged into one. The cemetery is the flyover. The flyover is the cemetery.

According to urban legend, this might not be the only motorway structure that doubles up as a burial ground. The Humber Bridge, for example, is said to contain the bodies of workers who fell into the concrete mix as it was being poured and could not be recovered. And there are many other rumours of bodies encased in bridges and flyovers across the country. On a website forum specialising in Fortean events, an anonymous user shared a poem told to him by his grandfather.

> And I saw old Baws McCall
> from the big flyover fall
> Into a concrete mixer spinning round
> Tho it wasn't his intent
> He got a fine head of cement
> While he was building up and tearing England down.

The motorways of Britain were built largely by immigrants from Ireland, but also from the West Indies, India and Africa, alongside the Welsh, Scottish and English. It was hard work. A feat of engineering forged from the blood, sweat and tears of its exploited workers. No wonder, then, that we harbour dark fantasies about them physically consuming human beings. The myth that motorway bridges and flyovers are laced with the bodies of unfortunate builders recasts them as objects of sacrificial ritual in which the occasional employee must inevitably become entombed in the name of the capitalist project. The gods must not be angered by unnecessary disruption to the completion dates or there will be hell to pay.

As well as unlucky construction workers, flyovers and motorway bridges are said to contain the corpses of victims murdered by underworld mobsters, who allegedly take advantage of motorway construction sites with their fresh vats of concrete mix to dispose of their rivals. In Glasgow, the Kingston Bridge, which carries the M8 over the Clyde, was built in the late 1960s, a time when gangs were embroiled in a vicious war. It was said to be so full of bodies that the integrity of the structure was weakened, causing some of its supporting plinths to crumble. London was another notorious battleground for gang warfare in the 1960s, and the Chiswick Flyover is reported to be where some of the bodies lie, including small-time crook Thomas 'Ginger' Marks, shot dead in Bethnal Green by a member of the Krays' gang and then tossed into the foundational concrete gloop somewhere between Junctions 1 and 5 of the M4.

This was quite a grim blow to the reputation of the Chiswick Flyover, which had begun life with great razzmatazz when its first section was opened in 1959 by the voluptuous American screen siren Jayne Mansfield. She turned up in a limo wearing a skin-tight dress, brandishing gold-plated scissors, and told the assembled newsmen that it was 'a sweet little flyover'.*

---

* It was the death of Mansfield in a horrific car crash in Louisiana that confirmed for the author J. G. Ballard his notion that there was an erotic aspect to the celebrity car accident. This would lead to the novel *Crash* in 1973, a book preoccupied

At the fiftieth anniversary of that event, the actress Imogen Stubbs took on the headline role. 'I'm not exactly the natural successor to Jayne Mansfield,' she told the *Evening Standard*. 'I think they asked me because, like the flyover, I'm homely and getting on a bit.'[26]

'Homely' is not a word that people would have associated with flyovers in the 1950s, when they were hailed as futuristic and glamorous enough to have Hollywood actresses attend their openings. Nor is it a word that many would have used in the mid 1970s when the public turned against flyovers, bemoaning the concrete invasion that had blighted their towns and cities. Flyovers were considered to have brought catastrophe to urban communities, destroying homes, wiping out historical buildings and polluting the environment. But at the same time, as we have seen, they created weird new spaces onto which to project our dreams and nightmares: cavernous amphitheatres, towering pillars, subterranean tunnels and concrete islands. What were considered to be intrusive carbuncles in the 1970s would gradually become familiar thoroughfares and local landmarks. Human life crept into their recesses and chambers. They attracted bored youths. Graffiti artists. Sex workers. Drug dealers. Rough sleepers. Their smooth surfaces became canvasses for art, political slogans and guerrilla advertising. They played host to raves, parties

with the psychological effects of our automobile obsession and how our primal urges find expression in the technologies of the twentieth century. It was a year later that Ballard then published his flyover novel *Concrete Island*.

and drug exchanges. Children developed their imaginations beneath them. In some cases, the problematic post-war structure Ballard described in *Concrete Island* has been embraced, even celebrated.

At the conclusion of the fiftieth anniversary ceremony of the Chiswick Flyover, Imogen Stubbs planted a commemorative tree; a natural offering, just like the Extinction Rebellion shrine I had seen on the interchange of the M32. It was a sign that life can flourish on even the hardest of surfaces.

‖‖‖‖‖‖‖‖‖‖‖‖

As I walked forth one summer's morn
Hard by the A-road side
Where green saplings did adorn
The flyover great and wide
I spied a doll upon the slabs
With flowers in her hands
Her sadness in her looks surpassed
The misery of these lands

I took some tulips from my coat
And placed them at her feet
Neath this skyway so remote
The girl was pretty in her seat.
Darkness overspread us both
Shadow where there was sun
The rumble of invisible gods
Drowned the pleas of everyone

I said fare thee well, oh pretty maid
'Tis soon our time to part
With vows of plastic love I laid
My head against her heart
Then into the underworld I walked
Where walls were made of bones
The paths with words of warning chalked
And fairie voices moaned

6

THIN PLACES

BEASTS AND LEGENDS OF THE INDUSTRIAL ESTATE

In a cradle of hills on the south bank of the Firth of Clyde, twenty miles west of Glasgow, is the port town of Greenock. Once a simple fishing village, it became a custom house port in the eighteenth century, then a major administrative centre during the Industrial Revolution when Clydeside was the engine room of the British Empire, with shipyards, foundries and factories along its length. During the First and Second World Wars, the town's manufacturing prowess was harnessed for the production of torpedoes, and as the main assembly point for the all-important Atlantic convoys, it became one of the key links in the country's supply chain. And then, in the 1970s and 1980s, there comes a story familiar to so many other parts of Britain. Industrial decline. Empty warehouses. Closed businesses. Soaring unemployment.

It was not long into this troubled period that the first sightings were reported of a strange figure lurking in the tunnels, backstreets and alleyways of Greenock's industrial areas. He lived wild, ate rats and would leap out at people on their way home from the pub, like a Scottish Spring-Heeled Jack. One theory was that he was a 'catman' of the sort employed by shipping companies in the town's heyday to look after the stray cats that helped keep the rat population down. And – like one of those legendary Japanese soldiers fighting in the jungle long after the end of the Second World War – he was still carrying out his catman duties, keeping rats at bay, forgotten and unpaid by some long-vanished shipping company. An alternative version suggested that he was a Russian sailor whose jaw had been broken in a fight on board his ship before he jumped into the sea and swam to the shore at Greenock where he subsisted on scraps and any rodents he could catch, rendered mute by his injuries. Some conjectured that the 'Catman' was an escaped mental patient. Others that it was just a prank to spook drunks at night. Many believed that he did not exist at all. He was nothing more than an urban myth.

It was only in 2007 that Catman was first caught on camera in wobbly, grainy footage of Greenock's Lynedoch Industrial Estate, a scruffy mishmash of walled yards, depots and ware-houses sprawling up the slope behind the railway line where it was rumoured that staff from the bus depot were feeding the creature. The footage shows a balding, black-bearded man lying on his front on some gravel, his face and hands black with soot, as if he has just emerged from a chimney.

'There's my pal,' says a voice behind the camera, eliciting a thumbs up from the figure on the ground. 'How's the rat?'

In front of the bearded man is a dead rat. He picks it up, contemplates it for a few seconds, then bites into it.

'Catman, how did you end up like this?' asks the filmmaker.

The figure on the ground makes no sound. He scratches at the ground with his hands, the rodent swinging limply from his mouth, then stares at the camera with piercing white eyes.

Subsequently, there have emerged many photos of the same bearded man crawling through a torn wire fence or peering out from beneath a truck, mostly taken around Scott Street, otherwise known as Scott's Lane, a narrow pedestrian alley behind the bus depot at the upper end of the town's industrial sprawl. There are pictures of teenagers crouched by an oil-soaked Catman, their thumbs up, in the way that tourists in Gibraltar take photos with feral monkeys. Videos show kids chucking food into the undergrowth and gasping in horror as a hand reaches to grab it. On a Facebook page dedicated to Catman, a local recalls how 'after school we would dare each other to stand next to his hole for a picture and out of the darkness you would see the whites of his eyes'.[27] Despite this, many locals continued to maintain that Catman was a myth and that these videos and photos were fabrications while others worried that he was real and in desperate need of help. Social services sent a care worker to find him, but to no avail. The police were informed, but could not find enough evidence to pursue the case.

It might seem astonishing that a crypto-humanoid creature can exist in the middle of a busy Clydeside town, but this belies the mysterious nature of industrial estates and trading estates. They conceal as much as they reveal. Behind brick walls and steel fences are muddles of yards and units, parking areas, hangars and warehouses. The boundaries can be hard to define. Some businesses have signs that indicate who they are and what they do, but others tell you nothing about what they are making, or selling, if anything at all. Who is in charge? What demarcates one territory from another? What is really going on? The estate operates with its own rules and logic, none of which are obvious to the outsider. They reverberate with clangs and crashes, hissing and drilling, from unseen activities, as incomprehensible shouts drift over the razor wire. A stench of gas assails us, and we assume this is part of some working process and not cause for alarm. Fires burn and we assume there is a reason for them. A figure watches us from a doorway and we assume that they must work there. But we don't really know and we tend not to investigate.

In *To the River*, an account by acclaimed writer Olivia Laing of her journey along the River Ouse, one passage describes her reaching the industrial fringe of Newhaven, where there is a 'scrapyard filled with crunched-up cars and glittering mountains of rusting metal . . . furnished with all manner of funnels, chutes and holding tanks'. She cannot comprehend what the place is for and whether it is abandoned or not. She adds: 'These places that are outside the human scale maintain anyway their own kind of invisibility: the eye drifts past them; their purpose is mystifying and their workings hard to name.'[28] Viewed this way, the industrial estate is arguably an ideal place for someone like Catman to disappear.

In 2016, Catman became the subject of a short film written by Chris Moar and directed by Graeme Edmiston. 'He's no like me or you – he's wild,' says a man in the film, who is dressed as a clown for reasons that go unexplained. 'He looks after the cats . . . that's why they call him the catman . . . he lives amongst the bushes.' Another interviewee claims he saw him in a tunnel and asked if the rat was all he had to eat, to which Catman nodded, unable to speak because of something awry with his tongue. When approached by the filmmakers, Inverclyde Council said that while the council would intervene in genuine cases where a vulnerable person was at risk, 'this would appear to be an urban myth'. The film also interviews Paul Bristow from Magic Torch Comics, who is fascinated with local folklore and has based some of his comics, short films and performances on the Catman legend. For Bristow, the story taps into our instinct for primal myth: our urge to create fictional narratives about where we live, then pass them down from generation to generation as a form of cultural preservation. In 2017, there was even a campaign to recognise Catman's 'contribution to the history and mythology of our town' by renaming the roundabout near the industrial estate the Catman Carousel.

Whether founded on truth or not, Catman is a contemporary Greenock legend, whose mythos will continue to grow. He was not the first legendary resident though. Many centuries before Catman arrived, the town was supposedly the birthplace of Captain William Kidd, popularly remembered as one of history's most notorious pirates. Born in 1645, Kidd was originally a sea merchant who became a privateer on the payroll of the British government, charged with defending shipping routes in the West Indies, while relieving foreign ships of their precious cargo at any opportunity. He was a legitimised thief, backed by a cabal of wealthy landowners and politicians. When public opinion soured against such privateering, the practice was outlawed in 1698, leaving the hapless Kidd on the wrong side of the law, and his backers with no inclination to help him. He was arrested and condemned to death by hanging in London in 1701. On the first attempt, the rope snapped, so they strung him up again, and after he was dead, he was dangled in a gibbet over the Thames for two years. Rumours about his hidden booty, based on a fictionalised confessional ballad that grew hugely popular after his death, became an inspiration for Robert Louis Stevenson's novel *Treasure Island* and the short story 'The Gold Bug', by Edgar Allan Poe, turning Willam Kidd into the archetypal mythic pirate.

In reality, though, Kidd was simply an agent recruited for an economic system based on the exploitation of foreign countries' resources and that rewarded violent trade protectionism, only for his masters to scapegoat him when they realised the game was up, literally leaving him to rot in full view of the public. Similarly, Catman, the 'lost' dock worker gone feral, was a cog in the post-war industrial machine that exploited the working classes for the economic benefit of corporations and politicians; discarded, when the jig was over, and left at the mercy of unemployment, hardship and mental health problems. Kidd and Catman are both victims of sorts, emblematic of their historical period, who have been transformed into something outlandish and fearsome in the popular folk imagination. This is never more apparent than in the short film, *Catman's*

Greenock, by James K. Beaton and Leo Bruges (2018) which uses the long-suffering vagabond to portray the town's post-industrial decline.

> Living, breathing like slaves, piled higher and higher on top of each other, getting spoon-fed processed foods, watered-down knowledge, 'I told you it was power'. The whole place used to be loud with employment and shipbuilding mastery, now it's been silenced into a whimper, of pain and poverty.

In this context, rather than a beast to be feared, Catman was more of an urban Robinson Crusoe, marooned on an industrial estate, the final vestiges of the beleaguered port town, while all around him had succumbed to demolition and redevelopment.

〰〰〰〰〰〰

The more I learned about Catman, the greater my desire to visit his lair and see if I could find any traces of him. After a short journey west from Glasgow to Greenock, I parked my car at Morrisons and walked beneath the Victorian railway bridge towards the outer wall of the Lynedoch Industrial Estate. Signs competed for my attention: Westburn Autos, Inverclyde Autosales, Cleaning Supplies 4U, Stop 'N' Steer Tyre Centre and Little Stinkers Dog Waste Removal Service. The air was alive with the hiss of jet-washers, the chatter of radio, the clang of steel, and the throb of a truck's idling engine. I followed Dellingburn Street as it ran up the eastern side of the estate towards a patch of greenery at the top of the hill where the road terminated. I passed the entrance to the coach depot, a prefab crowned with barbed wire looking onto a yard where, allegedly, workers used to feed Catman. Then I continued up the hill towards Scott's Lane, alongside a section of stone wall, blackened by exhaust fumes, dandelions sprouting through the cracks and a weathered metallic sign that read 'Greenock Welding'. As I turned to look back down the slope, I could see across the railway, beyond Morrisons and the marina, to where the Firth of Clyde sparkled blue and hills rolled on its northern shore. Now that I sensed the proximity between trading estate and dockland, I could imagine Catman crawling from his waterside origins, through tunnels and alleyways, sewers and sidings, to hide in this older place, where the developers were not yet flattening everything for retail and leisure.

At the upper reaches of Dellingburn Street I arrived at the entrance to Scott's Lane. This was Catman's lair, an alleyway with wire fencing on one side, and the side of a large industrial building on the other. The asphalt had been worn away at one side, exposing the cobbles beneath. It was quiet but for the sound of rustling leaves and traffic moving on Baker Street at the other end of the alley. Nobody passed me as I wandered up and down its length, probing the fence, beyond which was an unkempt jungle. In some places the wire had been cut, then peeled outward to create an opening. Other sections had been patched with corrugated-iron panels, some of which had bent to create new doorways. Outside one gap was a Tesco bag with damp clothes and a McDonald's coffee cup inside. Was this an offering to Catman? Above the bag, a pair of torn leggings were caught in razor wire. Perhaps the result of Catman's violent rejection of that same offering? It was all so open to interpretation, with the possibility of Catman's presence transforming the alley into something wild and frightening. I imagined him lurching from the bushes, coated in grime, hungry and desperate. If I was grasped by oily hands and dragged into the undergrowth, nobody might ever know.

Eventually, I plucked up the courage to enter the scrubland, ducking beneath branches of sycamore and ash, feet cracking on twigs. The ground was littered with cans and carrier bags, newspapers, soggy tissues and car tyres. Tubs of industrial paint were dotted around at intervals, as if strategically placed. I passed a smashed computer monitor, broken paving slabs, mouldering office furniture, an upturned shopping trolley and a pile of gas cylinders. This unkempt woodland had no apparent terminus, but I assumed it stretched down the slope towards the bus depot. Fallen trees had created caves, furry with moss, roots dangling from above, or had toppled into each other to create accidental bivouacs. Exposed rocks were slippery with algae and the air was dank. I found a large leather wallet full of loyalty cards. As I pulled out a Boots Advantage card to look for a name, I felt and then saw a cold white paste, like solidified duck fat, on my fingers, and I jerked back with a cry, dropping the wallet. It was pathetic, but my nerves were jangling. It was as if I were stalking the Yeti on an isolated Himalayan mountain, not lurking in an alley on a Scottish industrial estate.

Then again, I wasn't sure of the difference. While it had none of the physical remoteness of the Himalayas, this woodland behind the fence in Scott's Lane had as much psychological remoteness, being so close to society and yet so far away from it. Nobody comes here unless they want to take drugs, discard stolen goods, fly-tip rubbish, or have sex. It is a forbidden urban wilderness where a disabled man could feasibly subsist on rats and discarded McDonald's scraps while surrounded by streets and businesses, without the authorities being able to reach him. I had the feeling that I was exploring a porous threshold between the visible world and an otherworld beyond physical reach, like those 'thin places' in Celtic folklore where the spiritual intersects with the earthly, in which can be glimpsed gods, ghosts and monsters.

||||||||||||||||

With their liminal qualities, industrial estates can become places where the lines between human and beast are blurred, particularly in those edgelands where cities and towns fray into an uncertain semi-rural wilderness. While Catman is an example of a human who has morphed into an animal in the leafy nooks of an industrial estate, in the north of England there is an example of an animal that has taken on human form. In 2016, the *Huffington Post* ran the headline: '8ft Tall Werewolf "Old Stinker" Prowling In Hull Industrial Estate'.[29] There had been several supposed sightings of this beast lurking in the industrial fringes of the city, most recently at the Barmston Drain, a water channel that runs south through the city before discharging into the River Hull. The story was also picked up by the *Daily Mirror*, which shared the account of a woman who saw the werewolf bounding on all fours along the bank. When it came to a stop, it reared up on its hind legs then vaulted over a fence and ran up an embankment where it vanished into some allotments. In another account, a couple claimed they saw the beast feasting on the corpse of a German Shepherd dog. As they moved closer, it bounded over an eight-foot-tall fence with the dog still dangling from its jaws.

Paranormal experts have linked the sightings in Hull to the legend of 'Old Stinker', a werewolf from the Yorkshire Wolds, reports of which date back to the eighteenth century. There were wild wolves in Britain until the 1500s and Yorkshire was their final enclave, which could explain the persistence in local folklore of a half-dog, half-human hybrid – an expression of our primal fear of wolves, or perhaps our regret about their disappearance. Dr Sam George, organiser of the UK's International Werewolf Conference, believes that Old Stinker represents 'our collective guilt at the extinction of an entire indigenous species'.[30] Whatever the reason, Old Stinker was back, and he had strayed from his old haunts to take up residence, like Catman, in the industrial outskirts of our modern urban world. Charles Christian, author of *A Travel Guide to Yorkshire's Weird Wolds*, explains why this might be: 'By their very nature, old industrial areas offer plenty of places to hide and if there is something there it will know its way around. It would be the perfect habitat for a predator.'[31]

For his long-form poem *Flood Drain*, Tom Chivers walked the route of Barmston Drain as an 'attempt to trigger an altered state of consciousness', a process inspired by the medieval poem 'Piers Plowman', whose narrator has a vision after he lies beside a flowing river. The result is a dreamlike drift through a landscape of factories, wrecking yards and sewerage works. Studying the polluted drain with its floating trash of polystyrene and glass blooming with algae, Chivers writes 'the Barmy drain is full of death & death becoming life again'. At one point, heading towards the Stoneferry Industrial Park, he spots a creature hunkered next to the water:

> 'My god is that a bear?
>
> > my god
>
> is that a man in a bearsuit?'[32]

As he gets a closer look, he realises that the animal is in fact a horse chained to a post. But his fear that it was a bear is indicative of how the unease experienced in industrial edgelands can inspire visions of wild beasts. Such creatures seem to fit so naturally into these places that there are similar stories across the country.

In the run-up to the 2012 Olympics, the former industrial heartland of the Lea Valley in East London was reputed to have become the lair of a crocodile. It was said to lurk in the River

Lea near Stratford, where construction for the games was in full swing. It preyed on Canada geese, dragging them beneath the surface in front of shocked narrowboaters, leaving no trace except for prints in the banks at low tide. There were many rational explanations – perhaps it was a terrapin or mongoose, for instance – but hysterical newspaper articles kept returning to the crocodile myth.

By that time, I had been exploring this industrial landscape for three years and I believed that the story of the phantom crocodile said something important about what had happened to this part of London. The River Lea was once a wild, free tributary of the Thames before heavy industry spread into the lower valley and subjugated the river to its will, canalising stretches, adding locks and docks, polluting it with oil. Now it was under a new type of pressure from property development as the old warehouses and factories were torn down and luxury flats rose along its length, bringing hipsters, city workers, pleasure cruisers and tourists. Yet, despite all this, parts of the river remained in which traces of the past could be glimpsed: a darting kingfisher, a spawning fish, the moon's reflection on the rippled surface of the river as it meandered through areas of marsh unchanged since the Ice Age. To my mind, the River Lea was part of the city's reptilian brain, bearing memories of an antediluvian world of rhinos, elephants and wild cats that existed long before any human settlement. This notion that it could contain a crocodile was perhaps – like Hull's werewolf – a manifestation of regret for what had been lost.

The same area of the Lea Valley was also the hunting ground for a phantom bear, first spotted by a group of boys in Christmas 1981 while snowballing on Hackney Marshes. After they ran in terror to their homes, there ensued a frantic search by police on horseback, with helicopter support. They found some unidentified prints and a smashed allotment shed but no bear. The sighting was given some credence by the fact that only weeks previously, two skinned and headless bear corpses had been fished out of the Lea, perhaps linked to a visiting circus that regularly used the marshes as a pitch. Over the decades there have been other sightings of bears in the area, always glimpsed, never fully seen or photographed. That was until 2012 when a student spotted a large furry creature moving in the undergrowth beside the river. Her first instinct was that it was a bear. She took a hurried photo, which ended up in the local papers, only for it to be revealed as a Newfoundland dog, which in a slightly bizarre twist turned out to belong to the drummer of the 1990s indie band Kula Shaker.

I believe that these cryptozoological visions are so often linked to semi-industrial landscapes because they are a frontier between the city and wilderness; between present and past; dual states that inhabit the same terrain, discombobulating the mind. They trigger a primitive fear, conjuring up images of wild beasts occasionally emerging from cracks in time, blinking in the light, hungry after their long sleep, the scent of human flesh in their nostrils. In the same way that Tom Chivers momentarily glimpsed a bear in Hull, folk who walk in the Lea Valley leap to preternatural conclusions when something moves suddenly in the trees or the murky waters. A primal horror is activated beyond their control, just as humans have experienced for centuries when confronted with a foggy moorland, an ink-black cave, or the gloom of a wooded grove.

||||||||||||||||

There is a rich legacy of horror and violence connected with industrial estates. Accidents occur with alarming regularity, and they have a particular tendency to erupt into flame; possibly not surprising given there is so much explosive potential in their container gases, flammable liquids and stores of timber, clothing and paperwork. Often the buildings lie derelict or untended, leaving them vulnerable to arson for the purposes of insurance claims, revenge by business rivals or as entertainment for bored teenagers. These are just a handful of the incidents that took place in the first six months of 2019 alone:

> An Ocado warehouse burst into flame on an industrial estate outside Andover. Nearby homes and businesses were evacuated because of the risk of poisoning and further explosions.

> A fire caused by arson in the Bridge Road Industrial Estate in Bristol saw three hundred containers go up in flame.

> Huge smoke plumes rose over Sunbury, Surrey, from a fire at a trading estate in Hanworth Road.

A ball of flame exploded from a unit in the Blackpole Industrial Estate in Worcester.

A warehouse fire broke out in Golden Triangle Industrial Estate in Widnes. Two pre-teen boys were arrested on suspicion of arson.

Mayhem and violence are so synonymous with industrial estates, they have become a fictional trope and are regularly used as settings in television crime series such as *Line of Duty*, *Life on Mars*, *The Sweeney* and *Minder*. Wheeler-dealers in sheepskin coats meet in electric-fire-heated prefabs to discuss dirty business as the corpses of murdered associates fall into car crushers and men with crowbars chase each other across piles of rubble and batter each other to death on rickety iron stairwells.

In *Doctor Who*, the industrial estate is often shorthand for troubled futures or alternative apocalyptic presents. A 1970 episode, 'Inferno', with Jon Pertwee as the Doctor, tells of a drilling project to exploit a new source of power beneath the earth's crust. When the Doctor is accidentally hurled into a parallel universe, he sees the effects of this drilling, which has unleashed catastrophic heat and poisonous gases, not to mention green slime that turns humans into creatures known as Primords. The location for this stricken Earth was the Kingsnorth Industrial Estate in Medway. In a more recent episode, 'The Poison Sky' (2008), David Tennant's Doctor faces the Sontarans, who have implanted ATMOS devices in cars that unleash a toxic gas that will create an atmosphere conducive to their colonisation of the planet. Scenes outside the beleaguered ATMOS factory, as the world fills with smoke, were filmed at Usk Valley Business Park in Wales.

This fiery legacy has seeped from fact and fiction into ghost lore as well: in 2015 on the industrial estate of Aston, Birmingham, a photo captured a face staring from the window of a store for car parts, owned by scrap-metal business Taronis. It wasn't the first unsettling experience on the site. Workers claimed that when they entered the room, the temperature plunged and they'd hear sudden loud bangs. On one occasion, a toilet above the haunted room was found smashed, but there was no sign of a break-in and the alarms remained untripped. The manager told the *Birmingham Mail*: 'We've been here six years and when the previous owners visited, their first question was, "Have you seen the ghost?"' A medium posted her verdict on the company's Facebook page explaining: 'It's a boy, such a sad soul. He was very hungry and left to fend for himself. He got trapped and burned in a fire.'

The eeriness of these sites makes it easy to believe there are supernatural powers at work, In Ipswich in 2018 a young woman and her two kids were tormented every night for months by the disembodied voice of a child singing the nursery rhyme, 'It's Raining It's Pouring', which seemed to be emanating from a nearby industrial estate close to the railway. 'The first time I heard it, it was the most terrifying thing ever,' she told the BBC. 'I went cold and felt sick, and thought, "What on earth was that?"' The sound was like a crackling old gramophone recording and would strike up every two to three minutes. If it wasn't for her children being able to hear it too, she would have questioned her own sanity. Eventually she called the council. Although they were sceptical, they sent a team to investigate the eerie noise and eventually found the source of the music to be a loudspeaker attached to the side of an industrial building on the Farthing Road Estate. The recording was activated whenever the motion sensors were triggered, with the aim of frightening intruders. But the cause was neither intruders nor ghostly children. The recording was being set off by spiders crawling across the camera lenses, and the nursery rhyme was carried in the wind through residential areas.

While there turned out to be a perfectly rational explanation for the spooky music, it is a stark reminder that while we have built over fields, woodland and marshes with factories, roads and houses, what lay beneath has not gone. The urban world is not our sole domain. Hundreds of species of arthropods, insects and spiders live in our buildings, feasting on dead skin, nail clippings, mould and crumbs. Countless microscopic mites hide in our skin follicles and feed on our oily secretions at night. Inside our intestines, we are more bacteria than human. This is the horrific reality that people can happily ignore until the spiders of Ipswich's Farthing Road Industrial Estate, amplified by electronic sensors, become nightmare nursery-rhyme transmitters that wake us up with a start in our beds full of lice, sweaty faces seething with tiny monsters.

||||||||||||||||||

If industrial estates can leave us teetering on the border between the urban and the wild, so too can they act as the kind of 'thin places' that we have encountered before – narrowing the threshold between the past and the present. Like other late twentieth-century structures, they do not erase all that has gone before them; the histories of these locations are preserved in layers beneath the surface, like mosquitoes trapped in amber. And sometimes these stories can break through to haunt the present.

Martin Fuller is an amateur filmmaker who loves to explore the industrial areas of London. To an accompaniment of woozy electronic music, his films often feature subjects such as canals, locks, railway sidings and pylons all shown in lingering shots interspersed with bursts of psychedelic colour and noise. In particular he likes to film where the River Lea flows through Bromley-by-Bow. There it becomes Bow Creek before emptying into the Thames near the Isle of Dogs peninsula, which hangs like an elderly man's testicle from the undercarriage of Poplar. Once a dirty dockland, the Isle of Dogs is now home to Canary Wharf, which is dominated by the glass tower of One Canada Square, its pyramidal apex blinking like a Cyclops' eye.

When Poplar and Canning Town were industrialised in the late nineteenth century, housing was constructed for the influx of workers, not only from London but from the Caribbean, West Africa and Asia, creating one of the city's biggest multi-ethnic communities. But poor water supply and sewerage saw the area decline into slum conditions, and with clearances in the 1930s followed by Blitz bombing in the 1940s, it never quite recovered. As the shipping and freight industries disappeared, industrial estates and business parks have spread across the docklands, intermingling with parts of dockland that have barely changed since the 1960s: residential streets, working-class pubs and clubs that harbour the grimy legends of yesteryear. Now even these lingering fragments are in danger of obliteration thanks to a £1.7 billion regeneration project, which promises brand-new luxury flats and retail developments.

Martin wants to capture these final remnants on film before they are gone. For him, this is not an ugly backwater but a place that evokes his youth; a Britain of scrapyards and bomb sites, pubs with carpets and jukeboxes, where you could get a cheap drink and an honest day's work – or a dishonest one if the wind happened to blow that way. Like Jane Samuels' passion for the 1970s crack-house time capsule in Manchester, Martin sees the industrial docklands around Bow Creek as a portal to another era, a lost world that coexists with the new, for now, at least.

One of his favourite spots is Bromley Hall Road in Poplar, an area of salvage businesses and knacker's yards, piled with mat-tresses, tyres, corrugated iron, air-conditioning units, reclaimed wood, and rubble sacks. Remarkably, Bromley Hall itself still exists, a fifteenth-century manor house, which has accumulated layer after layer of past lives as a printing works, gunpowder factory, charity home, carpet warehouse and, finally, offices. It's an unlikely survivor on a wedge of land between the A12 and Bow Creek, obstinate against the flow of time. It was around here that Martin took me when we went for a walk, starting down Ailsa Street and Lochnager Street, between scree slopes of baby buggies, fridge freezers and office chairs. There were skips stacked up along the muddy lane, as if waiting for a larger skip to take them away. Behind a landslide of junk stood the building of a company that manufactured Indian and Pakistani clothing; a bricked-up window had the words 'SNACK BAR' engraved on the stone lintel from the days when this was a bustling place of work. Now its time was almost up. This whole area was about to be redeveloped into flats. 'Everyone must have been kicked off in the past few days,' said Martin sorrowfully. He clambered into the cab of a broken HGV with flat tyres and pretended to drive with childlike glee as I took photos, his face distorted by the spider-cracked windscreen. The only other soul we saw was an Afro-Caribbean man pushing an empty wheelbarrow, like Wall E, the lonely robot tidying up the trash on an abandoned earth.

On the other side of Bow Creek is a business park that includes the major distribution centres of large corporations, including Amazon and Sainsbury's, as well as the offices of Screwfix, DHL and Union Hand Roasted Coffee. Overlooking the scene are the wrought-iron skeletons of Victorian gasometers from a time when this was the site of the Bromley-by-Bow Gas Works. In a wedge of trees at the top of the business park is a memorial garden with an idiosyncratic array of features: a statue of Sir Corbet Woodhall, one-time Governor of the Gas Light and Coke Company; a columned rotunda, ornately detailed; a stone pergola containing a memorial for workers who died in the world wars; and a gas lamp that is permanently lit. The garden was in a poor state, littered with crisp packets and plastic bottles, a smashed television and a broken umbrella, its significance as a memorial fading in the public consciousness. In front of one of the trees I was surprised to find a small corroded brass plaque on a wonky wooden post, only shin-high, which read:

'This "ailanthus"– the tree of heaven – has been planted in memory of Andrea Schofield, born 3.11.68, died 29.11.87.'

Memorial plaque beneath the tree of heaven.

This tree had been planted in the shadow of dead gasometers to commemorate a family's grief in a once popular spot, but now stands in a barely tended memorial garden in the corner of a business park, dwarfed by corporate warehouses with high fences and CCTV cameras, the access roads rumbling with delivery lorries. I wondered if the family still came to this spot to mourn, over thirty years on, congregating at the plaque to a chorus of air-brake hisses and grinding gears. When a spot is chosen to commemorate a loved one, we imagine it will remain that way forever and cannot envisage those future upheavals which might alter the terrain around it. If the spot becomes forgotten, does that mean the person is forgotten with it? I believe that the contrary is true. Perhaps, every now and then, a random visitor to one of the distribution centres will stumble on this tiny plaque during a break from deliveries, full of amazement at the discovery of a secret garden. They might pause for a second to think about the person Andrea might have been, and why she departed this earthly realm at such a young age. In that moment her spirit will flicker alive again, like the gas light on the nearby pillar, in the mind of a total stranger from another century. There is a wonderful magic to that, I think.

Beyond the Amazon distribution centre, Bow Creek snakes along beneath Canary Wharf, the skyscrapers contrasting with the tumbledown plateau of the docklands. On the waterside is a sculpture by Abigail Fallis of a double helix spiral made of shopping trolleys, a giant twisting lattice silhouetted against the grey sky. Its purpose was to raise awareness of muscular dystrophy (the discovery of DNA by Watson and Crick was crucial to our understanding of the condition), but it was also about how consumerism has become entwined in our DNA – the perfect monument outside a business park. Hers is one of a sequence of artworks along the river, including pieces by Damien Hirst, Antony Gormley and Martin Creed. Further along we came to Cody Dock, which has been reclaimed by local artists as a sensory garden; it is furnished with decking, raised beds and driftwood benches.

In the adjacent art centre, historical photos of dockland workers reminded me that this mass of trading estates and business parks was once part of a huge international operation, unloading and loading goods onto ships bound to and from the corners of a colonial empire. Much of the labour was carried out by the multi-cultural community who lived in Canning Town, on the other side of the creek. Its once thriving residential areas are overlaid with knacker's yards, recycling businesses, cab firms and spare-parts dealers. Behind walls piled with tyre stacks, diggers crawl on mounds of earth. The noise of crunching metal fills the air. The asphalt is so threadbare in places that cobbles and old tramlines show through.

The threshold between eras here is porous. It remains a place where Hasidic Jews can enjoy a 'schmeissing' at the Docklands Steam Baths, London's 'last authentic bath house'[33] and where metal heads can see bands at the rock venue Bridge House 2. The original Bridge House, which used to be located a few hundred yards further south, was a legendary music pub in the late 1970s and early 1980s where landlord Terry Murphy hosted gigs by The Damned, Stray Cats, Chas 'n' Dave, Squeeze, Billy Bragg, Dire Straits, Iron Maiden and Depeche Mode. Its days as a venue ended in 1982, when the building was pulled down to make way for the A13 flyover. A little further up the same street is Pier One Nightspot – Nightclub and Grill, one of the first London venues to specialise in African music. It is not the only example of fringe music cultures flourishing in such places. Grime music originated above a nightclub on the edge of an industrial estate in Waterden Road, Hackney Wick, the secret location of influential pirate radio station Déjà Vu. Its remoteness kept it relatively safe from probes by the authorities, while the scene lasted. There is no physical trace of that night-club now. As journalist Dan Hancox points out, by the time grime pioneer Dizzee Rascal returned in 2016 for a live concert, 'the industrial estate had been replaced by the Queen Elizabeth Olympic Park and the crumbling East Cross Centre had been replaced by the £44 million Copper Box arena'.[34] A similar fate has befallen the original Bridge House pub in Canning Town, and may well put an end to all underground music in Bidder Street.

Back in Canning Town during the daytime, there were not many signs of life in Pier One Nightspot, surrounded by wheelie bins, its windows and doors shuttered. Also closed for business, but permanently, was the Durham Arms on Stephenson Street, a notorious haunt of gangsters, where nefarious deals were worked out over cheap pints. When the pub was put on the market in the 1990s, the Metropolitan Police jumped at the chance to take it over, hungry for information about the criminal underworld. They set up a covert operation, hiding microphones beneath the tables and fitting a camera in the dartboard. However, regulars somehow cottoned onto the ruse and any covert talk was concealed by the playing of Motorhead's 'Ace of Spades' on the jukebox at a loud volume. So the story goes. Martin used to pop in for a pint, and listen to the squawk of the parrot above the bar as its last few regulars smoked in defiance of the law. But now it is closed down for good – at least as a pub. This bastion of wheeler-dealer dockland culture has become a creative hub run by the Ministry of Startups offering hot-desking facilities and a cafe to help support nascent businesses – a development greeted with sporadic attacks of vandalism by some of the locals who see it as part of a hipster invasion. Of course, small creative businesses and artists are only the outriders of the rapacious property development boom in London: creatives, artists, nurses and students driven by overheated property prices into areas of cheaper rent, only for property developers to follow them there and drive them out again.

As we passed under the A13 flyover, Martin and I encountered yet more attempts to 'revive' the area – an installation of colourful steel plants and flowers commissioned in the run-up to the Olympic Games to make the route more inviting to walkers, tourists and cyclists. 'Visions of public access to the river that came to fuck all,' said Martin. An attempt to prettify this area won't eradicate its unruly spirit, not until the entire place has been bulldozed and turned into flats. Even then, its spirits might linger on – like Catman, Old Stinker and the phantom crocodile – glimpsed in the right conditions, in the right state of mind.

Industrial estates are the contemporary version of thin places where the border between the past and the present is unusually fluid. I think this is particularly true in locations where the earth meets the water: in London by Bow Creek; in Hull along the Barmston Drain; in Greenock by the Forth of Clyde. These are unsettled interzones, where the ghosts of the past can break the surface of the present, and living people can become like ghosts, trapped in the past. In the relentless drive for redevelopment and gentrification industrial estates like these teeter on the brink, haunted not only by the land-scape that came before, but also by the spectre of their own annihilation.

||||||||||||||||

As I walked forth one summer's day,
To view the waterside green and grey
A sudden movement I espied
Fast and fearsome by the river side,
And in't a human I heard shout
Alas! alas! The monster's out

Then round the warehouse did it stalk,
Beside the alley where I feared to walk
With cobbles from a time before,
The steel, the coal, the iron ore
And as it leap'd the wall I cried out
Alas! alas! The monster's out

Beneath silos of the foulest scents
Where pretty flowers grew through the fence
Something lurked and fed on rats
It wept, it sigh'd, it screeched like a cat;
Alas! alas! we all cried out
Alas! alas! The beast's about

7

CONCRETE CASTLES

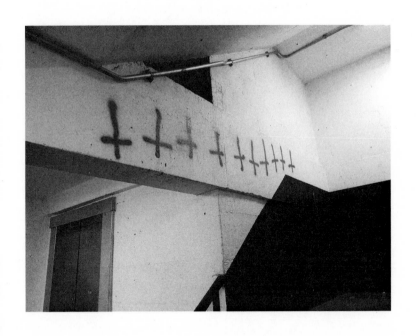

LIFE AND DEATH IN THE MULTISTOREY

The idea of visiting Harlow struck me while heading south on the M11 after a trip to Norwich. I was hungry, with time on my hands, and there was nowhere I needed to be anytime soon. Instead of stopping for a service-station sandwich I thought I might as well head to somewhere I'd never been. Exit signs with the names of historical rural market towns – Mildenhall, Saffron Walden, Bishops Stortford – flashed by, but they did not sway me, sounding as they did like rare cheeses or posh actresses. However, Harlow seized my attention. A new town in Essex, built after the Second World War as a London spill-over, it hangs in the greenbelt outside the M25 orbital, a landscape of tower bocks, elevated walkways and multistorey car parks, dreamed up by planners in the grip of post-war utopianism.

I exited the motorway and drove through a flatland of rich greens and yellows, baking under a midsummer sun, high-rises growing in the distance. The traffic slowed on the approach to a roundabout, which then slung me towards Terminus Street Car Park, built in 1975, one of three multistoreys in Harlow town centre. Looming above it was Terminus House, a fourteen-storey office block that has been turned into flats, exploiting a 2013 law change that allows developers to convert business premises without planning permission. London councils have since relocated hundreds of people to Terminus House, leaving them in cramped conditions above a multistorey car park, far away from their communities, in what has been described as 'human warehousing'.[35] But I had no idea about this legacy as I drove beneath the dangling chain portcullis of the 'maximum height' strip and through a raised barrier into the car park interior. My eyes struggled to adjust to the dimness as my radio crackled, and signal bars disappeared from my phone, as if I had entered a lead-clad bunker beneath the earth where no radio wave can penetrate.

The multistorey delivers a singular driving experience you don't get anywhere else. The floor surface is so smooth it's as if you are gliding on ice as you follow painted direction arrows up ramps with tight turns and no margin for error. You keep a lookout for the rear lights of reversing cars, or children dashing out, only milliseconds away from a catastrophe of flesh and metal, your knuckles white with the trace thrills of driving *inside a building* as if you're in a madcap movie car chase. At that moment, you are in all the different multistoreys of your life, stretching back to when you sat in the back seat and watched your mum or dad navigate its turns, tingling with that frisson of excitement that children experience when going through a dark tunnel. You might not realise it, but the multistorey is in your veins.

After all, multistoreys are not *new* structures. The first was built on Denman Street in London as far back as 1901. During Britain's post-war redevelopment the open-sided concrete multistoreys we know today proliferated across the country to become highly visible outposts of the new automotive reality, which would significantly reshape our towns and cities with ring roads, roundabouts, motorways and retail parks. In his book *Concretopia*, John Grindrod writes: 'Concrete itself is made from our oldest construction materials – sand and rock – and in the structures it was used to create in the twentieth century there are echoes of some of our building traditions – castles, catacombs, cathedrals, monasteries, walled cities, watch towers.'[36] Like the castles that permanently altered the British landscape after the Norman invasion, the brutalist multistoreys have gone from intimidating carbuncles to familiar sights, growing old, leaky and worn over time, as loved by some people as they are loathed by others.

Getting out of my car in the Terminus multistorey, I shivered in its chilly microclimate as I headed to the pay-and-display machine, surrounded by the familiar soundtrack of clunking car doors, sputtering exhausts and disembodied human voices, amplified by the hard surfaces all around me. Instead of going downstairs, I took the stairs up a few floors to take in the view. The stairwell gave the impression of being hundreds of years old, worn by millions of feet, stained with piss and phlegm and sperm and beer. On the ceiling, rusted iron poked through patches of broken concrete, bleeding orange tears. Liquid seeped from cracks in the wall. Thick cobwebs obscured the plastic light coverings. It felt as if the car park was collapsing under the weight of its experience, the process of slow ruination laid bare, with no render, wallpaper or paint to disguise it. When I reached level 3, I leaned on the edge and gazed out across the jumbled flat roofs of Harlow's town centre, framed by tower blocks and rival multistoreys, crumbling to dust beneath an unforgiving sun.

On leaving the car park, I was surprised to find that a section of the lowest level was occupied by a Mecca bingo hall. In an outdoor space enclosed by railings and a bed of Yucca plants, women perched on stools, heads bowed over blue games machines. I was less surprised to see several bunches of fresh flowers tied to the railings a few metres away. They were positioned close to a permanent steel memorial plate designed in the shape of a gravestone and dedicated to a man who had died in January 2009.

It is not the first time I have seen flowers outside a multistorey. In my home town of Hastings, a teenager fell to his death from the shopping centre car park and for weeks the lamp post near the spot was festooned with photos, poems and floral tributes. These structures have a natural attraction for the impulsive suicide, with their vertical precipices and unyielding tarmac beneath, offering certainty of death. They are easy to access at any time of day or night, and few of the drivers inside will notice what you're up to until it's too late, focused as they are on getting in and out without a scratch. Who would even notice your expression of distress in the dim interior? To another car-park user, you are just a faceless body. A movement in the half-light. A shadow within shadows. Glimpsed briefly but never truly seen until you are up on the ledge. There are so many stories of car-park suicides, they could fill endless sad pages. A nineteen-year-old leaps off a car park after taking LSD . . . A depressed businessman jumps to his death . . . A coke dealer throws himself from a ledge the day before his trial . . . A husband jumps after his marriage breaks down . . . A woman with seasonal affective disorder kills herself after she switches medication . . . These incidents happen every month, which is why many stairwells and lift doors in multistorey car parks are now adorned with Samaritans helpline posters.

When I was a teenager, I overheard someone tell my mum about a friend of theirs whose son had jumped from the top of a multistorey. He had given no warning. Friends and family had spotted no symptoms of depression. There was no note. No evidence that he had planned it in advance. It was as if he had decided one morning that he wanted to end his life, then simply walked off the edge of existence. I never dug into the details or spoke to Mum again about the story, but the tale has lingered for decades like a ghost story heard in childhood that leaves a permanent scar, or a bad dream I cannot forget. I was haunted by a mental picture of the young man, compelled by an urge he could not resist to climb the cold hard steps of the nearest multistorey and take his own life. I didn't need to know the details of the car park's location or a description of what it looked like. Multistoreys were as familiar to me as tower blocks, pylons and cooling towers. In my mind's eye I had a clear image of a mottled concrete layer cake on which there stood a figure of man on the uppermost ledge, silhouetted against a grey sky, a step away from oblivion.

With this tragic legacy, there is little surprise that car parks can feel haunted. In a Glasgow multistorey in 2008, a driver saw a woman cross the car park, clamber onto the edge and jump, but when they went to inspect, there was no body, or evidence that anyone had fallen.[37] In 2017, the *Sun* reported a 'TERRIFYING ghost who haunts a car park'.[38] CCTV footage showed a girl with long black hair in a white nightdress walking past a wall, before appearing to become absorbed into it. Her close similarity in appearance to the girl Samara from *The Ring* films suggests that it was a hoax, but the choice of a car park as a setting shows that the multistorey has become a place of inherent creepiness in the public imagination.

There are plenty of tragic deaths to inspire sightings of spectres in multistoreys, but in some cases, the story is about what lies beneath the foundations. For instance, Dundee's Bell Street car park is reputedly haunted by a sobbing young girl. It was built in the 1960s on the site of a nineteenth-century cemetery, where an estimated 10,000 bodies are interred. Some of the original tombstones remain visible, built into a wall adjacent to the car park, one of which is said to be that of the ghost child.[39] In a 2016 YouTube video, Jag Betty, a musician, poet and urban philosopher, went hunting for ghosts in the car park using Echovox, a smartphone app that claims to pick up spirit voices. Sitting in his car within the gloom, Jag asked his phone a series of questions. 'Hello', he said. 'Is there a sobbing girl spirit here, please?' A chaos of noise fragments crackled from his phone. He strained to listen. 'Hello?' he said again. 'What's my name, please? Who am I? What am I doing here?' From the sonic jumble, Jag picked out the phrase, 'lots of bodies' and 'north of Dundee' but admitted, 'I really am messing with things I don't understand.'[40]

In Bell Street the gravestones are highly visible outside the car park, showing the historical function of this place as one of grieving; perhaps this is what inspires visitors to feel that it is haunted. I wonder if the increasing phenomenon of car-park suicides will have a similar effect over time – the proliferation of Samaritans posters, memorials and flowers ingraining the structure with morbidity in the common imagination, to the point that we might subconsciously associate them with the dead, in the way we might a church graveyard.

The gravity of a religious site predating the car park can pull on your imagination when you are in it, especially when that ecclesiastical function is still ongoing. For instance, in my dad's home town of Wrexham, North Wales, the St Mark's Road multistorey is on the site of a Methodist church, demolished in the 1960s to make way for a brutalist concrete shopping centre. As part of the redevelopment, a replacement church was integrated into the new building. Its concrete steeple juts onto the street between Shoezone and Poundstretcher, a silver spire and crucifix poking up above the multistorey. As I explored the stairwells of the car park one morning, I found graffiti of upside-down crosses sprayed with red paint. This same paint had been used for a nearby pentagram – a five-pointed geometric star sealed within a circle, used as an occult symbol by Wiccans and pagans. In a multistorey fused with a church, was this a mockery of Christ, the daubings of an alternative multistorey church or something else entirely? As I ventured deeper into the car park I was enthralled by the weirdness of its physical decay: ectoplasmic green paint smeared on fire doors; fossilised blobs of chewing gum; reinforced glass coated in some kind of slime mould, which gathered in pools on the corroded ledge; Turin-shroud watermarks on the walls; outlines of objects that had long been removed. Even without the Satanist graffiti, it wouldn't take a lot of imagination to feel uneasy in this place.

Weird, creeping stains in the St Mark's Road multistorey.

With its cold shadows, shadowy nooks and forests of pillars, a car park can seem as uncanny as an ancient mossy woodland or a lichen-covered graveyard. But you don't need to tell that to many of the people who work in these places; they can feel it in their bones. Like Mark Hollis, who manned the sentry box at the entrance of the Nelson Street multistorey car park in Bristol during the mid 1990s. Mark was an aspiring artist with no interest in climbing a career ladder. For years he had skipped from job to job, happy so long as it paid a wage and gave him plenty of time to think. He particularly loved this new job at the NCP, despite the authoritarian attitudes of the top brass at the time, who were mainly ex-military or former police. Occasionally they would swagger through the car park in long brown coats, barking orders like characters from *The Sweeney* but they weren't a problem that Mark had to worry about too much as a nightshift worker, when he had the place mostly to himself. His job was to monitor the entry barrier, check the car park for suspicious intruders, and wander through the levels with a black plastic bag to collect up litter. Most of the over-night parkers were patrons of the nearby Grand Hotel, which meant that cars rarely came and went, giving him plenty of time to master *Road Rash 3* on the smuggled-in Sega Mega Drive that he would plug into the mini-TV on his desk. Occasionally, he would stare into the strip-lit interior, lost in his thoughts, where he'd see dark shapes swirling in the gloom, as if his eyes were swimming. The car park did not frighten him. Not at first, anyway.

One night he carried out his first inspection round as usual, then left the bin bag on the ground, a little way from his booth. With a contented sigh, he clambered back onto his seat to restart his video game. As he played, he noticed that familiar swirling darkness in the periphery of his vision, more intensely than before, but he thought nothing of it. A few hours later, it was time for his second inspection. But to his surprise, the bin bag he had left outside the sentry box was no longer there. Mark wandered around the few parked cars on the lower level, confused. He must have absent-mindedly left it in a different spot, but he could find nothing. It was only when he wandered up the ramp to level 2 that he saw the bag lying on the floor, as if hurriedly abandoned. There was no way he had left it there like that, he thought. Someone was playing a joke on him. Possibly, the other nightwatchman was having a laugh at his expense. Maybe it was mischievous teens, or a drunk who had wandered into the car park. That said, he'd heard no footsteps and, as far as he was aware, he was the only human being in the building.

Mark picked up the bin liner and proceeded through the levels, keeping a look out for anything suspicious, before he returned to the ground floor, where he once again dumped the bag in the usual place. In his booth he got ready to fire up the Mega Drive once again. But before he reached for the controller, an ominous sensation made him turn his head and look into the car park. He took a sharp breath. Around the bin bag seethed an inky black mass, thicker than the darkness around it, gathering itself around the object as if trying to haul it away. After a few seconds, it formed the shape of a large, heavy-set man. But after he blinked, it was gone. Mark trembled, the Sega controller wobbling in his hands. What had he just witnessed?

The next day, he met the other nightshift worker and told him his tale, not without a little embarrassment, expecting laughter in response. But his co-worker did not smile. 'Yep,' he said, grimly. 'I have seen it too. Not just once either. It happens a lot. I just didn't tell anyone as they'd think I was lying or crazy.'

Mark had sought an excuse to shrug off the incident but now that his friend had confirmed it, he was really spooked. For the remainder of his time at the Nelson Street NCP, he was on edge. He didn't mind the early part of the shift, when the car park resounded with noise from revellers enjoying themselves in Bristol city centre. But as things began to calm down after 2 a.m. – the exact time he'd first seen the bin-bag spectre – the atmosphere would change. The car park would fall deathly quiet, but for wind blowing litter through the levels, the drip of water in the stairwell, and the occasional shriek of a siren in the night. That was when he'd sometimes notice the warp and flex of an obsidian shape in the dark recesses and feel once again that primal dread.*

* This is the same Mark who, twenty-five years later, created *The Ghost Box* – the oil painting of Dungeness that haunted my waking nightmares in Hastings as my marriage collapsed and storm tides tore away the coastline on which the reactor stood, threatening the end of humanity. If the eeriness of Mark's painting had been inspired at all by his experiences at Nelson Street then perhaps this NCP multistorey was the true origin of my troubles.

There are few who, on their own in a car park in the late hours, wouldn't feel a twinge of nerves if they suspected that there was someone or something else with them in the building. Countless films and TV shows have used these atmospheric spaces as locations for confrontation, assassination, murder, rape. In one common trope, a young woman walks alone through a car park at night, heels clacking. Strip lights crackle, shadows flicker in the darkness of the parking bays, and the occasional glint of metal shines like a cat's eye. A sound startles her. The clatter of the lift doors opening. Footsteps. Steady at first, then faster, with purpose. She glances back but cannot see anybody. As she picks up her pace, so too does her stalker, the footsteps louder, faster. Now she has her keys in her hands, heart pounding, running to her car, where she fumbles at the lock in panic. As she opens the door, a gloved hand covers her mouth, silencing her before she can scream.

This damsel-in-distress cliché is challenged and dismissed by writer Clare Archibald in a piece called 'Contraflow' that she created for Walking Heads, an online venture that explores overlooked corners of Scottish cities. Archibald depicts herself entering a multistorey for no purpose other than to walk through it, cataloguing her impressions. While she admits that the stairwells might contain something potentially uncomfortable, she does not wear 'the clippety-clop high heels of the foalish, skittery victim' but walks with 'woven stealth' as she revives her memories of youthful days spent boozing in places like this with friends.

You'd take your turn of teenage swigs then run up and down the concrete ramps to increase the blur, lapping the long winding altars to the shops that leapt across the road. You were reckless. You sat in stairwells with boys.[41]

Teenage drinking is a quintessentially British rite of passage. Getting the oldest-looking friend to buy the Buckfast or White Lightning in the dodgiest possible off-licence. A stolen bottle of vodka from the family drinks cabinet. Spirits decanted into a bottle of Coke. That joy of intoxication and where it can lead – first kisses, clumsy fumbles and other inaugural transgressions, where the carpeted cosiness of your parents' home seems far away and their rules no longer apply. Multistoreys are a popular location for such teen gatherings. Under cover of concrete you can skate, you can run, you can shout, you can hide, you can seek, you can drink, you can puke, you can smoke your lungs out and you can scream at the top of your voice. These teenagers are the unruly spirits who haunt so many of our high-rise car parks. In St George's multistorey in Stevenage, drivers regularly complain of kids smoking weed, skateboarding on the ramps, boozing in the stairwells, starting fights, and even holding a party inside a lift.

Head to Northampton's Grosvenor Centre multistorey and you can see across the Boroughs, the medieval heart of Northampton, to where the castle once stood. That castle might be gone, but on the roof of the car park, contemporary knights joust with Fiat Puntos, VW Golfs and Ford Fiestas in late-night car rallies, showing off their under-lights and dump valves. Scrawled over the turquoise-green surface are black rubber tyre marks in crazy loops and figures of eight. The multistorey as unofficial sports arena.

Then there were the kids I encountered in Grimsby's Abbey Walk multistorey. A couple of boys came running up the concrete spiral ramp, sound-tracked by grime blaring from a phone speaker, and whizzed past me, howling 'they're coming, they're coming' before hammering at the lift buttons, looking anxiously behind, embroiled in a semi-fictional adventure. The perimeter wall of the roof deck was sprayed with a pair of breasts, crazy eyes emoji, and the word JOYRIDAZ. Someone had filled in the faces of the painted pedestrian stick figures on the ground, adorning them with eyes and grinning mouths. The kids who use this multistorey understand this terrain in a way that no paying customer does: the length of time it takes to traverse a floor; the best hiding spots; the perils of sheer drops; how fast a car can take its corners; the feel of concrete grooves against their skin. In the slow time of a child, where reality is constantly refashioned, even the plainest surface can become weird, funny and mysterious. A car park is a blank space on which they can project their imagination. They can be in a gang. They can pose on the stairwell and pretend they're a band. They can tell tall tales about their exploits. They can be king of the castle. They can become someone else.

But it isn't just bored kids who are drawn to multistoreys; these places are the refuge of all those with nowhere else to go. Addicts cast out by their families. Alcoholics who swap tales during a night out of the rain. In Swindon, in 2016, no fewer than four car parks – Parade, Brunel West, Fleming Way and Whalebridge – contained encampments for the homeless, with mattresses and camp beds, transforming them into semi-permanent places of refuge. Nikka Pomponi, representing the homeless charity Threshold Housing Link, told the *Swindon Advertiser*: 'Our hostel is nearly always full, which is probably why some of these people can't get a space.' The typical response to these kinds of endemic social problems is an attempt by the authorities to push the victims somewhere else by closing multistoreys at night or, in one case in High Wycombe, deliberately pumping repetitive noise through the car park to force out rough sleepers. But who is to say that the nocturnal inhabitants are not the rightful inheritors of the space?

In the introduction to their anthology of essays, *Consuming Architecture*, Daniel Maudlin and Marcel Vellinga argue that buildings do not have fixed functions dependent on the intention of architects and planners. They are in a constant process of occupation, appropriation and interpretation by those who inhabit them. They quote Arjun Appadurai's work of anthropology *The Social Life of Things*, which proposes that objects can go through different phases of life, with different meanings and values for the disparate groups who dwell in and around them. It is what a building is used for, day to day, that makes it what it is. This is true of the multistorey, an open-sided, all-access local landmark that many feel is a common space, even though it's privately owned. A mourner laying flowers. A ghost hunter with his sonic device. A teenager taking an acid trip with friends. A homeless man taking shelter. A graffiti artist with a can of spray paint. Me, wandering around, taking notes for a book. We each consume the car park in our own ways and, in doing so, change it. Unleash its latent potential. Reveal its inner poetry. Transform it into something more than a concrete income generator.

North East Lincolnshire Council believes that anti-social behaviour in the Abbey Walk car park is putting off customers and is seeking investment for a refurbishment programme. But it might not make a difference. Multistoreys are an old solution to an outdated problem. Shopper numbers are falling in town centres as more of us shop online or visit retail parks. Many multistoreys are now underused. In central London many are becoming obsolete as heavy traffic and congestion charges reduce demand and some, such as the Welbeck Street multistorey, have been demolished. A campaign spearheaded by the Twentieth Century Society tried to save the building for its architectural qualities, but to no avail. Jo Underhill, a photographer who documented Welbeck Street's final years in her project 'Ode to Welbeck', said, 'I love the harsh geometry and alien appearance. It would have been great to see it repurposed rather than completely demolished', adding that not only was it aesthetically interesting but 'historically important and an important part of the community'.

And there is plenty of scope to find new uses for them. Repurposing car parks is becoming a popular idea in an era where pubs are closing, high streets are struggling and spending cuts have decreased the availability of public spaces such as libraries, youth centres and sports fields. In some towns the multistorey is already fulfilling a social function as a playground for bored kids. Others have been transformed into playgrounds for adults, such as the one in Peckham that was saved from demolition and repurposed as an arts space with a rooftop bar called Frank's Café. The top three floors played host to exhibitions and cultural events, including a performance of Stravinsky's *Rite of Spring* by the Multi-Story Orchestra. If operas, plays and concerts can be performed in castles, which were once pragmatic military compounds, why not in multistorey car parks? They might be cold hard objects of necessity but they also have a place in our collective memory as sites of tragedy, refuge and rites of passage; with a capacity to inspire fear and awe.

In a new reality of pandemics and global warming, where we must rethink our behaviour when it comes to shopping, entertainment and travel, who knows what these bastions of infrastructure might become? They might linger in neglected parts of town, like ruined Norman castles, eroded to stumps by the weather, unofficial memorials to the age of the combustion engine. Or they might become something else entirely – citadels of poetry, music and cinema, where people gather on chilly evenings, holding hands, breathing curls of steam, to dream new ways of living.

ıııııııııııııı

By yon car park wall, at the close of the day,
I heard a girl sing by the pay and display,
And as she was trilling, my ears they could tell
She lamented the loss of a loved one who fell

'The world's in ruins, we all know the cause
Extinctions, pandemics, and murderous wars,
We daren't say it is true, but we all know it well,
Yet none of it matters since my poor Jamie fell'

He was on the top deck at the break of the day
A ghost on the concrete, his face it was grey
The demons they took him right under their spell
And shed not a tear when five storeys he fell

'The world's in ruins, we all know the cause
Extinctions, pandemics, and murderous wars,
We daren't say it is true, but we all know it well,
Yet none of it matters since my poor Jamie fell'

8

THEATRE
OF FATE

Mortuary Visitors
Parking Only
in the Blue Box

A HOSPITAL
ANTHOLOGY

My recollection of my first daughter's birth is a fragmented drama set in Homerton Hospital in Hackney. We had wanted a water birth with low lighting and ambient music, because it sounded the most pleasant option in our NCT classes, but things soon went wrong and we were pushed into a room with a machine that went 'ping'. Twelve hours later, my wife had received three failed epidurals while bonged to the gills on so much pethidine that she started to speak like Keith Richards, amid a constant flow of blood and urine, but nothing would stop the pain, or the yelling. In the mayhem my expertly curated ambient electronic iPod selection was drowned out, not only by my wife's screams but those of other women, echoing through the corridors, and I was forced to switch it off. By two in the morning, all of her efforts had come to nought and she was wheeled into the operating theatre and cut open while a radio blared The White Stripes' 'Seven Nation Army'. It was as if my wife was a car that I'd taken to the mechanics. I'd never seen an operation outside of TV shows, where they were usually performed to a soundtrack of bleeping electronic music with dramatic stabs of violin, so the FM radio rock sounded strange blended with the knitting needle clack of incision tools. Eventually, my daughter was removed from her exhausted body without a whimper, her skin eggshell blue, and I was ordered to hold a tiny oxygen mask over her face, staring in love and terror until some colour flushed into her, to my indescribable relief.

No birth can happen without incident. Clumsy conceptions. Bizarre food cravings. Waters breaking in the worst place at the worst time. Dramatic races to hospitals. Fathers missing the birth for hapless reasons. Hilarious swear words cried out during labour. Emergency Caesarean sections. Babies on ventilation machines. Moments of tenderness. When we later tell the story, we pick only a fragment or two, condensing the tale into a vignette, polished for a more palatable sheen. This then gets passed down to your child as a form of family folk tale: your personal version of the Nativity. For most, the stage set for this tale is the modern hospital, a building about which you might have no awareness until, suddenly, it becomes the hub of your anxieties, fears and joys, all played out against the clinically neutral decor of polished floors, white walls and clunky machines.

There are infinite possibilities for breakdown, disease and decay that might lead us to a hospital. A fractured leg. A change in your bowel movements. A headache that won't go away. Arthritic pain. Rogue bacteria in the gut. A relative gets ill. A child is rushed into casualty. A partner needs an operation. Whether the ensuing events last twenty-four hours or twenty-four months, the hospital dominates your world for that time, becoming rich with melodrama, its white surroundings saturated with technicoloured emotion. In a ward cubicle, a human life can end or begin, with all the grief, horror, love and beauty that this entails. Epic moments that will forever resonate in our lives. But immediately after the event, the sheets are changed, the machines removed and the surfaces wiped down for the next patient. The cubicle is restored to a blank canvas with no sign of what has occurred; only the memories of those who experienced it, and the story they tell, remain, both of which become embellished and refined over time, until they are as much figments of the imagination as real events.

That story might be only one of a hundred that occurred in that hospital that day, each one as unique as a snowflake even though they shared the same commonplace backdrop. In this way, a hospital is more a mythical construct than it is a physical place. Its floors, walls and corridors are conduits for grand narratives that extend through time and space, often surviving longer than the life of the building itself.

In my own Nativity story, it was stuffed peppers that heralded my coming, rather than an archangel. My dad was a Welsh soldier and my mum was a Scottish teacher. They had met in Germany where she was working at a forces school. In the late summer of 1973 my dad was on exercise in Northern Ireland, while my mum saw out the end of her pregnancy in Gütersloh. She was at her friend Gail's flat, eating those spicy stuffed peppers, when she got what she thought was indigestion. This turned out to be the first pangs of labour, which she realised only once Gail had left for work and the contractions began. Mum phoned an ambulance, which rushed her to the army hospital BMH Rinteln, fifty miles down the road. The military didn't let soldiers on exercise break their radio silence, so Dad was oblivious to events in Germany while my mum gave birth to me with no support other than the midwife, who told her that she should stop yelling with pain because she was an officer's wife and 'not a Woolworths shop girl'. The midwife went on to inform her that she was off duty at 5 p.m. sharp, so Mum had better hurry up and deliver the baby. And it was precisely 5 p.m. when I entered the world, which might be why I have always been a punctual person, or so my narrative goes. We hunger for signs of cause and effect because it helps us interpret the chaos of existence; perhaps this is why creation myths are fundamental to almost all civilisations.

In later childhood, if I ever mentioned that I was born in Germany, it would send other kids into impressions of a goose-stepping John Cleese from the famous scene in *Fawlty Towers*. I wasn't ashamed of it, but neither was I German, so I had to qualify the statement by adding that it was 'the *British* Military Hospital'. This gave BMH Rinteln more importance in my origin story than most would usually attribute to their hospital of birth. I recently Googled the hospital to find out what it looks like today and was surprised to find it featured in an article entitled 'The World's Creepiest Abandoned Military Sites'. A video showed Alan Legge, the former hospital Sergeant Major, strolling down its corridors, opening swing doors to shine his torchlight on beds, gurneys and wheelchairs. It was startling to see the building in which I was born depicted as the sort of site from which an urban explorer might post photos of his trespass on Instagram amid a flurry of shocked-face emojis.

Abandoned hospitals are popular 'Urbex' targets because of their eerie quality. Dusty windows cast their light on rows of beds and broken technology, discarded gowns and surgical gloves – lonely relics of a place that had been once so intense with life and death. It is easy to imagine the cries of newborn babies. The nail-biting fears of people waiting outside operating theatres. The urgent shouts of medical staff. Touching reconciliations. Final words. Last breaths. Moments of enormous significance, which cannot help but leave their mark, even after the bloodied bandages and needles have been cleared away and the surfaces disinfected.

These moments can resonate even after a hospital closes down, which could be why so many are said to be haunted. After Barnes Hospital in Greater Manchester closed in 1999, nightwatchmen reported seeing movements in the windows and glimpses of patients in the wards.* After it closed in 1994, Nottingham's Mapperley Hospital went on to be used as the set for ITV medical drama *Staying Alive*, only for the filming to

---

* Barnes Hospital was one of the settings for the 1974 Spanish-Italian zombie film *Let Sleeping Corpses Lie*, also known as *The Living Dead at Manchester Morgue*. But during the hospital's working life, there really were reports of the dead coming to life. Nurses reported a number of strange incidents, including a phantom nurse in 1940s clothing seen taking the temperature of invisible patients, and one occasion when a patient was seen fully dressed and making his way to the exit, despite having died in the hospital the previous evening.

be disrupted by unidentified shrieking. When it then became the headquarters of the Nottingham NHS Trust, staff reported hearing voices calling their names and the spectre of a woman in one of the corridors. There is a similar story in Liverpool's Newsham Park Hospital, once a nineteenth-century orphanage, sanatorium and morgue before it reopened as a hospital in the 1950s. Since its closure in the 1990s the building has fallen into disrepair, luring in ghost hunters who claim to have heard children's voices. Whether these are extant spirits or not, it is easy to understand why abandoned hospitals inspire visceral sensations of pain and loss in their visitors; even in empty operating theatres and dusty wards, the raw emotions of past experiences inflame imaginations.

BMH Rinteln was only the first of many hospitals in my life. There was the Manchester hospital in which I lay as a child with an ultrasound device pressed against my chest, investigating a suspected heart murmur; the Staffordshire hospital where I waited grumpily as my dad was treated after snapping his Achilles heel in what would be his last ever local rugby match, his beloved pastime terminated by the shake of a doctor's head; the Wrexham hospital where I visited Nana after she was taken ill; the hospital where I was X-rayed after a persistent chest infection; the Hastings hospital through which I ran, clutching a vial of my semen, which I had been told to 'produce' at home, then get to the correct department within thirty minutes, instigating a thrilling if slightly bizarre race against time. But most vivid of all was my strange experience of St Thomas's Hospital in south London, where I was taken after being hit by a car outside Stockwell tube station when I was twenty-five years old.

I have no recollection of the moment of impact, only that I woke up with surprise to see the night sky above me, the back of my head cold and wet, as if I was lying on a pillow of ice cream, and a metallic taste in my mouth. The roofs of shops and the sides of tower blocks in my peripheral vision flickered with blue lights, which looked very pleasing until I realised that they were cast by the ambulances and police cars that were here for me and that I was in serious trouble. By the time I fully comprehended that I had been run over, I was being hoisted into the ambulance on a stretcher, then driven to A&E, where the hospital was a fragmented collage of images seen from my prostrate position on a stretcher, pain roaring in my head, terrified that I was dying. I remember very vividly that the square panels of the ceiling above reminded me of my primary-school canteen, which could have been because they really did look similar, or because I was having a warped near-death flashback to my childhood. When I try to recall that ceiling now, I have no idea if what I can see in mind belongs to the hospital corridor or the school canteen.

In the cubicle my bloodstained clothes were thrown on a chair as I was hoisted into the air by paramedics checking for spinal damage. Then I was wheeled to an MRI scanner, an imposing cube of slightly dated-looking sci-fi machinery in the centre of a large room. I was placed onto the tongue of the scanner like a communion wafer by priest-like staff in white coats, then drawn into the whirring machinery while they muttered comments and pointed at screens. From there, I was taken to get my skull X-rayed, in what looked like an old boiler room with flaking paint and grub-like pipes curling from the ceiling corners. Then it was back to my cubicle where a nurse stitched the back of my head together. In my memory she was the clichéd Irish nurse, with red hair and a singsong voice, but I am not sure whether that's really true. For the duration of the seventeen stitches I fixated on a framed picture of a Venus Flytrap hung on the wall. Such an odd artwork to have in casualty. A flesh-eating plant. What was it supposed to represent? The indiscriminate jaws of fate? The circle of life and death?

In times of drama, details like this emerge that you would not usually notice so intensely: the sound of the swing doors; the smell of the ward; the pictures on the walls; the nasal hair of the doctor looming over you. What appears at first an impersonal space becomes the theatre of your fate. With your future in the balance, the sensory impact of such details becomes magnified and refracted by the emotional lens through which you are viewing them. This is particularly true when you spend a protracted amount of time in the hospital as an inpatient, outpatient, or visitor. In Owen Booth's novel *What We're Teaching Our Sons*, he describes the scent of the phenols used in hospital floor cleaners and anti-bacterial bandages, commenting that at some point in our lives, 'everyone ends up getting to know that smell, ends up associating all sorts of memories with it. Like they end up getting to know the pattern of tiles on the floor of at least one particular hospital corridor from walking it, again and again,

waiting for news.'[42] In *Walking Stumbling Limping Falling*, a published email conversation between writers Alyson Hallett and
Phil Smith, Hallett describes a three-week period spent visiting
her ill mother in a hospital where she herself had once spent
weeks recovering from hip surgery. 'The hospital corridors are
very familiar to me,' she writes, 'like old friends.' She continues:

> These walks are strange walks. As soon as I'm making
> them, I'm also wishing I wasn't. The fetid air. Incumbent
> germs. The compulsory scoosh of antiseptic hand gel before
> entering a ward, hands wet and glistening. The landscape
> is irrepressibly right-angled. All of it. Every possible curve
> ironed out. Staff wander by in strange uniforms. Odd paper
> hats on the heads of men and women who work in the
> theatres. Gurneys squeaking here and there.[43]

Though Alyson is forced to trace the same route through an
ostensibly bland building, her imagination enlivens even the
most mundane micro-details. Noticing that the green non-
slip rubber surfacing on the stairs has little raised circles in it,
she wonders 'if circular insects might have burrowed into the
material when it was being made, and now live in their strange
universe on the hospital stairs, getting beaten down each day
by the footsteps of visitors'.

In a hospital you visit a certain bed, frequent a specific ward
or dwell repeatedly in the same waiting area, feeling ownership
of that space as it becomes increasingly familiar, right down to
the swirls in the abstract artwork on the walls. There is a sense

that the world of the hospital somehow revolves around you and that your personal drama is central to operations, which is how the wonderful staff of the NHS tend to make you feel. But while it might seem the most important, emotionally charged experience of your life, eventually the experience ends, in one way or another – with a cure, a recovery, a birth, a death. Then you leave the stage and the hospital continues to be the site of someone else's trauma. They sit in the same chair or the same bed, gnawing their fingernails just as you did, treading the same staircases and corridors, befriending the same nurses, receptionists and ward porters. You are only one of millions to pass through this space. And yours is only one of the millions of stories that make up the grand anthology of the hospital: an empire of memories too vast to collate and impossible to recall in their entirety.

||||||||||||||||

Some modern hospitals are made up of stories that reach so far beyond their walls that their mythology is better known than the buildings themselves. Founded in 1247, the asylum Bethlem Hospital was also known as 'Bedlam', which has since entered the language as a byword for chaos, disorder and confusion. In 1676, a new home for the hospital was constructed near Moorfields in a palatial building inspired by Louis XIV's Tuileries Palace in Paris. Despite the surroundings, the treatments given there were brutal, involving chained restraints, isolation, starvation, beatings and ice-cold baths. Wealthy visitors would pay to revel in the hospital's opulent architecture and ornamental gardens, but mainly to view the spectacle of the thousands of lunatics locked up inside. Then, in the nineteenth century, the hospital moved again, to St George's Fields in Southwark, where its reputation for severity continued.

Today's Bethlem Hospital opened in 1930 on the site of Monks Orchard House in Beckenham, South London. Detached red-brick buildings with well-kept lawns are arrayed along wide avenues. Woodland, orchards and fields are woven through with footpaths with benches and ornamental features. With its church, swimming pool, coffee shop, community centre, sports field and bowling club, it feels more like a English suburban town than a hospital. But its past is kept alive, even in this twentieth-century version. The hallway of the hospital museum contains the two statues that were mounted on the gateposts of the Moorfields site. One depicts a manacled man, his face contorted in a tortured cry, to represent mania. The other represents melancholy. Upstairs the gallery contains works by patients including William Kurelek's *The Maze*, painted in 1953 when he was at Bethlem's sister hospital, the Maudsley. It depicts the back of a man's head, opened up so that the viewer can see the mind, which is represented by a maze of rooms with a white rat in its centre. Each room contains symbolic images: puppets dancing; a horny bull; a bullied boy; a violent father; a victim strapped to a conveyor belt. These are all aspects of Kurelek's mental turmoil. Beyond him, the sun shines on wheat fields, which seems a pretty contrast to his turbulent mind, until a closer look shows a swarm of grasshoppers attacking the crop. Kurelek explained that this represented his father's cruelty to him as a child, which stemmed from 'his raging impotence in the face of farming failures'. Even the countryside is warped by his emotions.

Similarly, it is a peculiarity of the modern Bethlem that its bucolic grounds both conceal the minds of the people within the buildings and manifest them. The external walls of the occupational therapy department's art studio are covered in ceramic artworks made by patients in the 1990s: a ship of fools heading off the ledge; a pregnant woman riding on the back of a crawling figure, flanked by giant dancing babies; colourful wild animals; mermaids; a frieze of cats dancing to fiddle music; hand imprints like Stone Age cave art; clay heads pushing through a series of square windows with a myriad expressions of sadness and joy.

Fantastical beasts of the occupational therapy department.

Figments of the patients' imaginations spill out beyond the walls of the building, with green and purple snails leading past a courtyard garden created by staff and patients. Further away, on the grass near the cafe, the clay figure of a puckish boy clutches a penny whistle. These folkloric figures are reminiscent of the most famous artwork to have been produced at the hospital, *The Fairy Feller's Master-Stroke*, painted by Richard Dadd in the Southwark incarnation of Bedlam where he was committed in 1844 after he became so convinced that his father was the devil that he dismembered him. Beyond a mesh of briars, grass, nuts and daisies the painting presents an array of fantastical creatures, including satyrs, centaurs and the fairy king and queen, Oberon and Titania. The artwork was inspired by a speech in *Romeo and Juliet* where Mercutio describes Queen Mab, a fairy who rides at night through the minds of sleeping folk, filling their dreams with horrors, fantasies and lascivious desires.

The grounds of Bethlem are a medium for recovery through artistic expression, but some of its buildings conceal the darkest agonies of severe mental illness. River House is the forensic psychiatric unit for those who commit violent crimes and are too ill to be sent to prison. It is surrounded by high fences, clad in thick steel and overlooked by security cameras. Walking through the pretty orchard beside it, there is no sound from those inside, who have been removed from the world, unable to feel the grass under their feet, or smell the ripening apples in late summer. Dan Duggan, a former patient at Bethlem, has spent over a decade in acute mental health wards and relates his experience in a collection of poems, *Luxury of the Dispossessed*, in which he writes: 'I was inside four months, no trees / no fresh air, no sun but what I gathered / through locked windows.'[44] Just as eighteenth-century Bedlam's palatial architecture belied the pandemonium within, so the peaceful environs of modern Bethlem contrast with the tumultuous minds of its most tormented inhabitants as they battle with their demons.

Another building in Bethlem exists only in the memory of the few who ever entered it. In 1999, twenty-five-year-old occupational therapist Kirsty Otos and her co-worker Karen became intrigued by a rumour about the macabre contents of one of the outhouses in the grounds. There was strictly no staff access to the building in question but Kirsty and Karen wondered if perhaps the groundsman could be swayed into letting them in. To their surprise, it took only a little cajoling to get him to agree. With trepidation, they followed him towards the detached, single-storey brick building. He carefully unlocked the double doors and they stepped inside the darkness. Slowly, one by one, the strip-lights flickered on. The rumours had been true. Stretched out before them were rows on rows of wooden shelves packed with glass jars. And inside every jar was a human brain preserved in formaldehyde. Each jar had written on it, in elegant ink lettering, the name and age of the brain's previous owner, along with the date of their death. As well as whole brains, there were glass slides containing slices of cerebral tissue. How long these had been here, they could not be sure, but they guessed they were at least half a century old. Six months later, the outhouse was demolished and the brains were gone. When Kirsty talks to Karen about their experience in the 'Shed of Brains' these days, they wonder if it ever really happened at all, as if the rumour had only briefly become fact and then retreated back into the realm of speculation. Just another mythic story to add to Bedlam's centuries-old legacy.

IIIIIIIIIIIIIIIIII

A building full of brains might sound incongruous in a modern institution but hospitals contain many weird spaces. No-entry areas. Toxic zones. Locked rooms. Inexplicable machines. While exploring the fringes of the poltergeist-plagued Nunsthorpe Estate in Grimsby, I recall walking around the Princess of Wales Hospital. Outside the mortuary, protected by railings, I encountered a hideous metal vat, streaked brown and yellow, with a blood-red pipe attached at the top and another curving out from its flank. It looked like Max Ernst's 1921 painting *The Elephant Celebes*, inspired by a line from a German nursery rhyme: 'The elephant from Celebes has sticky, yellow bottom grease'. The artwork depicts a disturbing mechanical monster: part elephant, part bull, part corn bin. This felt similarly surreal. Something out of a nightmare. I could not work out what it was for, or why it was there. Perhaps it was a boiler. A repository of fats. Fuel for the incinerator. Whatever it was, it was an unnervingly visceral object, the sort that is usually tucked away where visitors cannot see.

On his website Anatomy of Norbiton, an exploration of suburban life in south-west London, author Toby Ferris describes his view of Kingston Hospital, which 'stands just over the horizon of Norbiton like a planetary mass . . . brick chimneys, metal ducts, slate roof; and to the left, concrete, glass and aerials'. For Ferris, hospitals are 'chaotic spaces on the margins of civilisation' and he goes on to explain why:

> Hospitals have no centre, they are jumbles of elements: little clinics, Victorian brick gargoyled with extension and annex and awning, Portakabins, assimilated streets of ivied houses, stacks of signs pointing to departments named for benefactors . . . For a hospital administrator, looking at the ground plan of his hospital must be like scientists at CERN looking at scattergram sub-atomic particles – the memory of a location, a best guess, a most recent intelligence.[45]

Under constant modification and improvisation, the hospital is unknowable in its entirety, even to those in charge, making it plausible that mysterious sheds of brains and vats of human matter can exist alongside the well-polished floors and signposted corridors without anyone knowing why. To test this notion, I decided to visit a hospital to which I had never been, with no illness, no appointment and no loved one within its walls. *What does a hospital look like,* I wondered, *when you don't need to be there?* Stripped of its emotional charge, is it still a weird place?

Northampton General Hospital stands east of the town-centre ring road in the Cliftonville area. My first encounter was with a grand, three-storey stone building on Billings Road overlooking a busy junction, where an alcove in the wall harbours a statue of St George above a bust of Edward VII with the engraving:

A WISE AND MAGNANIMOUS PRINCE A LOVER
OF PEACE AND AN EARNEST WORKER FOR THE
WELFARE OF HIS PEOPLE HE WAS DEVOTED
TO DUTY EVEN IN THE HOUR OF DEATH.

The cigar-chomping Edward ended his life with a flurry of medical conditions, including a stomach ulcer, bronchitis and several heart attacks. The reference to doing his duty 'even in the hour of death' comes from the story that on his final day of existence – 6 May 1910 – he refused to ail in bed, declaring, 'No, I shall not give in; I shall go on; I shall work to the end.' This 'work' included a series of fainting fits, during which he was told that his horse, Witch of the Air, had won its race at Kempton Park. 'I am very glad,' he said, falling unconscious for the last time, presumably pleased that he had been a conscientious thoroughbred horse owner to the end. It was the Liberal Party who were the true welfare pioneers during his reign. In a bid to fend off an ascendant Labour Party, they gave 13 million workers sickness benefit, free medical treatment and maternity leave – the first shoots of reforms that would eventually lead to the creation of the National Health Service, undoubtedly the greatest domestic political achievement of the twentieth century.

I crossed the frontage of the Victorian extension to the original Georgian building, replete with symmetrical windows and classical columns, then followed the track of a hedge to reach a wing with a pitched roof, colonnade and fancy cornicing. This was the surprisingly majestic entrance to Northampton General's sexual health clinic. A gate with ornamental wrought-iron heads, entangled in ivy, led me into the sprawling grounds behind the original buildings, where I could see the kind of modifications noted by Toby Ferris. Black prefab extensions with ventilation pipes curling around each other like giant, mating worms. Fan casings bolted to stone. Luminescent yellow handrails. Recycling bins, plastic grit containers and raised verges with the kind of cotoneaster shrubs you usually see in a supermarket car park. The oncology centre was a glass-and-brick Travelodge-style building, inside which I saw a row of elderly people hooked up to drips.

As I meandered deeper, I passed students in doorways, uniformed nurses and smokers huddling by the entrance bollards while police cars and ambulances cruised by. Eventually I reached a zone of silver ventilation flues and loading bays: that grisly area where hospitals dispose of scalpels and needles, bandages and gloves, body tissues and fluids. Set back from the road opposite the mortuary, the incinerator chimney was adjoined by a steel silo on the side of which was written BIO-INTAKE. But precisely what kind of biological waste were they turning into heat? *What were they burning in there?* I recalled rumours of the remains of aborted and miscarried babies being used to heat hospitals, an accusation later admitted by ten NHS trusts in 2014. My mind vomited up a horrific image of human fat, hair and sinew in heaps. It was the Grimsby hospital all over again.

Beside a razor-wire fence were cylindrical fuel tanks on concrete ramparts where I found discarded items arranged on a defunct air-conditioning unit: a plastic funnel; an unidentifiable red object wrapped in many layers of plastic; a piece of bent metal; a section of concertinaed venting duct. It looked like an experimental sculpture. Were these objects connected by a shared narrative or was this a random mix of items that had accumulated here over time? Perhaps they did not fit into the established categories of waste, so were abandoned in a moment of panic in a place where visitors usually don't look. If these objects could not be recycled in this zone where all manner of bizarre materials were converted into heat, then where could they go? Perhaps nobody knew and these things had been moved around the hospital from room to room, alleyway to alleyway, rubbish pile to rubbish pile, by generations of bewildered maintenance staff who had no idea what they were handling. In his novel *Jerusalem*, a fusion of historical and supernatural fiction about the mythos of the Boroughs area of Northampton, Alan Moore writes: 'Human existence is a grand recurrence. Nothing dies or disappears and each discarded condom, every dented bottle-top in every alleyway is as immortal as Shamballah or Olympus.'[46] If Moore's vision held true, perhaps these strange objects and I were locked together in an eternal loop.

On an adjacent road I passed the 'Blood Taking Unit' and entered through some double doors to find myself on a corridor with beige walls and grey floor, bordered by blue handrails. This was Hospital Street, a stream of ward porters, nurses, patients and officials heading with purpose in either direction. Occasionally the pedestrians diverged to make way for an oncoming wheelchair, before converging gracefully again like murmuring starlings. I had no idea where I was in the hospital but assumed that if I continued to the end of Hospital Street I would reach a main exit. But as I was swept along, I grew disconcerted at the length of the corridor, which seemed far greater than the length of any single building that I had passed on my walk. It began to feel as if the corridor was some kind of TARDIS and that I was lost not only in physical space but space-time too. Occasionally a junction led into a ward with its own reception desk, but I didn't want to ask for directions, being an imposter with no reason to be here. What would I say if challenged? Who goes into hospitals when they don't need to? It felt as if I was making a mockery of the place, strutting healthily past the sick, a dark tourist in a world of other people's pain, clogging up the system. But I pushed on regardless, sure that I'd reach a corner with a big fat arrow pointing to freedom.

However, as the human traffic thinned out I realised that I wasn't heading for an exit, but deeper into the medical heartland. Signs overhead identified departments with 'ology' words that I could no longer understand, for conditions that sounded as serious as the looks on the faces of the staff and patients, hugging each other or talking in close confidence. Behind each doorway I passed, people were suffering from complaints I had never heard of but that I might one day come to know all too well. These were the hospital stories that had not yet happened for me. It was like being in a hypochondriac frustration dream, wandering a never-ending corridor of progressively worsening possibilities towards an unknown end. Perhaps this walk down Hospital Street was no accident. Instead, fate was guiding me to my salvation, or my doom, in a subconscious drift towards a specialist ward for a disease I did not yet know I had. At any moment a doctor might take me by the arm and lead me into a room of bleeping machines where surgeons with scalpels and hacksaws would be waiting patiently by a leather-strapped gurney, so that the next story in my personal hospital anthology could finally begin.

||||||||||||||||

'I must be going, no longer staying,
This hospital I have to cross.
Oh, I must be guided without a stumble
Down its corridors of loss'

When he came to his true love's ward
He sat down gently on the chair
And in her ear he whispered slowly:
'My dear girl, are you there?'

She turned her head upon her pillow,
And sightless were her eyes
Saying: 'Who's here at my bedside
From which I shall never rise?'

'Oh, I'm your husband, please recover
I pray you let life back in
For we must leave this hospital
And its endless shrieking din'

'Not so,' said she, 'here's where I stay'
She spoke through bitter tears
'My soul lives forever in this empty place
For I've been dead at least three years'

He stood and looked about the ward
Its beds beneath grey sheets of dust
The gurneys empty, curtains torn
Left to ruin and rust

9

MEMORY
MOTORWAYS

AN EMOTIONAL LIFE
OF THE M6

A couple of months after my brush with death out-side Stockwell tube station I travelled to the Scottish Highlands with my friend Jason. After a boozy weekend among the Munros, we hit the road south, back to London, exhausted and hungover. Darkness fell as we hit the M6, leaving only balls of sodium-yellow vapour to show the way, the headlamp beams of Jason's battered Volkswagen Polo fizzing with rain as we bumbled along in the slow lane. At the signs for Lancaster we decided to take a pit stop to refuel with caffeine. We pulled into Forton Services and sat in the cafe, clutching strong coffees, looking across the motorway at its famous hexagonal tower, glowing like a spaceship in the night. Jason and I had been flatmates since I moved to London twelve months previously. I had no job and relied on getting the odd commission to write advertising scripts for local radio stations. Things were tight. We owed our landlord rent and there were piles of unpaid bills, all of which meant that not much investment had gone into the maintenance of Jason's car, which chuntered and spluttered asthmatically as we pulled back out onto the motorway. I put on a cassette of *Endtroducing* by DJ Shadow and gazed out at the dark topography as the beat of the music blended with the ferrous-tape hiss of tyres on the wet road. After a while, Jason started to shift in his seat.

'Gareth,' he said, 'don't freak out, but there's something wrong with the car. I don't have my foot on the accelerator but the car is speeding up. I'm using the brakes to slow us down.'

I laughed at what I thought was a wind-up but he pointed to his foot as he lifted it off the brake and waggled it demonstrably to show there was no contact. As the speedometer started to rise, the engine whining like an old biplane racing towards take-off, I could see that he was telling the truth. I was gripped with fear. Heart thumping, I tried to shake off the image of our contorted bodies being consumed by a fireball in a twisted cage of steel on the hard shoulder.

'What do we do?' I said. 'What do we do? What do we do? What do we do?'

'I don't know.' Jason hunched over the wheel, peering at the dashboard as if an answer might flash up on one of its analogue dials. The car juddered as the brakes strained to hold back the accelerator. I was sure I could smell burning. The stench of a Scalextric set that's seen better days. A metallic tang in my mouth like the blood I could taste when I woke up on the roadside in Stockwell. That car accident was only a trial run, I thought. This could be the real thing.

As time passed, our initial panic subsided into numb silence. It was like one of those scenes in a cartoon comedy where a character plummets down a deep hole, screaming in terror, but the hole is so deep that they keep falling and falling until they eventually stop screaming and resign themselves to their fate. Hurtling uncontrollably down the middle lane of the

M6, with plenty of motorway ahead of us, we settled into the unfolding catastrophe and tried to think logically. How could we stop the car? Could we simply turn off the ignition? What would happen if we did that? And if we couldn't start up again, what next? The problem was, we had no idea. We were utterly ignorant of how cars worked, which meant that everything we did in that runaway Volkswagen Polo was guesswork. My main worry was how much motorway we had left before we hit Birmingham, where we'd need to leave the M6, which would entail slowing down or stopping at an interchange if we didn't want to hurtle straight into a roundabout. Perhaps this was like the film *Final Destination*. Having survived my car accident in Stockwell, I was now being hunted down by a vengeful Death, angry at being cheated out of a soul. And of all the motorways on which I had to perish it would have to be the M6. My first motorway. My special road. My beginning and my end.

The M6 came into my life at the end of my second year in primary school, when my family moved from Kirkintilloch to Glossop. Of course, I didn't realise it was the M6 at the time. What child ever looks at road maps or considers the number of the road? You just clamber into the car and enjoy – or endure – the ride. For me, it was simply *the motorway*, a high-speed conduit that took us to England, through Carlisle, Preston and Manchester. For the rest of my childhood, it then became the route back north to visit family in the holidays. On those trips, after the initial thrill had drained away, my brother and I would resign ourselves to the passing hours. Mum's Gene

Pitney cassette would be playing, or Dad's mixtape of hits from the 1960s and 1970s, my brother and I chiming in on tracks such as 'Wigwam Bam' and 'In the Year 2525'. Occasionally, we'd perform puppet shows in the back window, or bicker over who was encroaching on whose seat. But mostly I'd stare out at the scenery rushing past, enthralled by the rhythm of flickering pylons, bridges and street lamps. After dark, electric beams of light would slice their way through the car interior in hypnotic tones of orange and yellow, lulling me into a trance. If we were lucky, Dad would pull into a service station – places that had something other-worldly about them, like restaurants in space, where burgers came with a carousel of sauces and the bags of sweets were gigantic.

When I was sixteen my Dad got a new job with an adhesive company in Stafford, and we moved to Shropshire. The M6 now formed the majority of our route to Scotland, further embedding it in my consciousness. It became a mental holloway, seared into my neural networks through sheer repetition, which is why it remains the one road that gives me a true sense of belonging, even though I have lived in the south of England for twenty years. On those rare occasions now when I drive up the M6 to Glasgow with my two daughters, they become me and my brother in the back seat, asking if we're nearly there yet, while I am my father, saying 'no' and turning up the volume on the stereo.

The M6 is not only where it began for me but for all motorways in Britain. It was the first one to open, beginning life as the Preston Bypass, a concept sketched out in the 1930s by James Drake, the Lancashire County Surveyor, pioneer of our national motorway network. It wasn't until December 1958 that it was opened by Prime Minister Harold Macmillan. A few years later came the Lancaster Bypass, followed in 1963 by the section running to Birmingham. When the northernmost stretch to Carlisle opened in 1970, the M6 as we know it was born. It snakes up through the Midlands to the North West, through cityscapes, industrial estates, retail parks, farms, forests and mountains, until it hits Gretna Green on the Scottish border, where it invisibly transforms into the M74. There have been plans to name the entire motorway, either side of the border, the M6, but such proposals meet with resistance from those who believe that its upper reaches should remain the M74 to maintain its Scottish identity. This goes to show that while the tarmac may be monotonous and monochrome, motorways can have a distinct cultural history, hewed as they are into a land of extant national borders, idiosyncratic natural features and historical sites, many of which determine its route and shape. They manifest in urban communities as bridges, underpasses and flyovers which have political and social effects on those places, creating weird new spaces for crime, art and hedonism.

The motorway is an important story in the lives of those who live near it, as we have seen with the Chiswick Flyover, the M4 in South Wales and the interchanges of the M32 in Bristol among many others. But a motorway is more than the object itself. It is the view it gives you of the topography and architecture through which it passes; the service stations you stop at; the exit signs that once led you to the homes of lovers, friends or family members long gone from your life; slip roads to the sites of holidays, weddings and parties in your formative years. A motorway is a conduit for dramas – whether they take place in the car or at the start or end of a journey: that time you argued with your partner, hitchhiked to a festival, or broke down on a wintry night.

Whenever I see signs for Lancaster on the M6, I get flash-backs to the time I sat with Jason in that runaway car. As we racked our brains for ways to stop without crashing or break-ing down, there eventually came the sound of a loud snap, the engine cut out and we coasted onto the hard shoulder. We waited for a while before deciding to try the ignition again. To our relief it started up and we slowly made our way back to London, stopping at almost every service station to give the car a rest. That memory is forever scorched onto that stretch of motorway so that when I drive along it today, I can still see Jason and me, hurtling along to the sound of DJ Shadow, grimacing in panic, unaware that we are figments in my memory, trapped like ghosts in a recurring echo of the past. If it were possible to manifest all of the significant life moments that have occurred on a single stretch of motorway, I imagine there would be an ectoplasmic cavalcade of crashes, prangs, pranks and arguments, singalongs, shock revelations, terror, rage and laughter.

This belies the popular notion of motorways as 'non-places', a term coined by French anthropologist Marc Augé in 1992 to describe homogenised spaces of transit, such as airports, bus terminals, hotel chains and superstores, which are detached from local culture and history. In *Carscapes*, senior investigators at English Heritage Kathryn A. Morrison and John Minnis describe how the motorway garnered this reputation very quickly, quoting the architect W. G. Howell in 1963: 'Unless you are a connoisseur of bridges, you could be anywhere from Watford to Preston.'[47] In more recent years, journalist Nell Frizzell described motorway service stations as 'modern hinterlands ... palaces of anonymity ... everywhere and nowhere; a non-place we've all been and nobody remembers'.[48] However, I believe that British motorways have distinct narratives, character and identities; and that the passing decades have transformed them from anodyne super-modern structures into entities with a rich emotional life and powerful resonances in our memories. But to find this out empirically, I decided to spend two days of my life travelling on a motorway with no ulterior destination, to experience it as a place in itself, not a route to somewhere else. There could be no other choice for me but the M6.

‖‖‖‖‖‖‖‖‖‖‖

It was a dark evening in early January when I approached Corley, the southernmost service station on the M6, where I had booked a room at the Days Inn Hotel. The going had been slow, thanks to construction works for the smart motorway upgrade, forcing me through an interminable vale of orange cones at fifty miles per hour flanked by mounds of churned earth where men in hi-vis jackets moved among the sputtering excavators. A sign reassured me that Corley was 'open for business as usual' and pointed me down a temporary slip road, where I entered an almost empty car park. Inside the main building, Subway and the Food Court were closed, leaving only WHSmith and Waitrose to offer me teatime snacks. I opted for a classic service-station Scotch egg and a bottle of red wine that I planned to drink later while watching television in bed. It seemed the right thing to do, alone on the M6, a week after Christmas, with only a meat-coated boiled egg for company. Exiting Waitrose with my bag of delights, I passed a 'caution wet floor' cone standing on dry tiles. An elderly cleaner in skinny black jeans and a woolly hat leaned against a dormant floor-polishing machine and scrutinised me, jaw slack, as I walked through the double doors and up the stairs to a covered luminescent green pedestrian bridge, where I paused a while to look through its dirty Perspex slots at the dazzle of headlamps below.

In the Days Inn, a cheery receptionist tapped my car registration into the database and handed me a plastic key card. I went off in search of my room, heading down a white corridor that seemed to go on and on, lined with identical brown doors, the fire-escape at the end telescoping away as if I were walking against the direction of a travellator. In unfamiliar hotels I always feel as if I'm in *The Shining*. Stanley Kubrick understood the inherent strangeness of corridors and exploited that in his set design for the film, positioning doors in a way that lacked logical sense, imbuing the scene with the subjectivity of a nightmare where any horror might lurk around the corner. The Days Inn had that sense about it. For instance, there were two identical box canvas prints placed side by side on the wall: 1970s-style horizontal brown and orange stripes against a yellow background that wouldn't look out of place in Kubrick's Overlook Hotel. Further along was another pair of prints, exactly the same, as if to trick guests into thinking they are re-treading the same piece of corridor. These artworks brought to mind a novel by Will Wiles called *The Way Inn*, which satirises the architecture of chain hotels. The protagonist, Neil Double, is a professional conference-goer and therefore a regular at Way Inns up and down the country. He gradually realises that the abstract artworks on the walls of each hotel form a larger piece that links together the many other branches across the world. As Double investigates this phenomenon, he becomes disorientated in the maze of unfolding corridors and repeated motifs, realising that they don't make physical sense. They transcend time and space. Double discovers that he can enter a Way Inn in one geographical location and exit somewhere else entirely. This nails the design aesthetic of chain hotels. They deliver the same experience in all of their branches, using colour schemes and artwork to smooth out the idiosyncratic wrinkles of locality. It was an inauspicious start to my trip. Only an hour into my expedition and I had passed from the M6 into the Kafkaesque universe of Wiles's novel.

There was yet more strangeness in the stairwell leading up to my floor. It was a framed poster, containing the Days Inn logo and the text:

> It's not just gravity that pulls you towards the sun.
> It's also free wi-fi.

I read it once. Then twice. And I was still confused about what it meant. So I read it again, this time having a mental play with the emphasis.

> It is not *just* gravity that pulls you towards the sun.
> It's *also* free wi-fi.

Like most people, I suspect, any mention of gravity makes me think about how it holds us on the surface of the earth. Of course, it does also keep the earth in orbit around the sun, but my hunch is that few people think instinctively on this planetary level. And in any case, this claimed we are being pulled *towards* the sun. A quick check on Google showed me that in 2004, Russian dynamicists G. A. Krasinsky and V. A. Brumberg calculated that the sun and earth are actually moving apart by fifteen centimetres every year – something to do with the gravity of the moon slowing the earth's rotation, which affects our solar orbit. So gravity is not pulling us into the sun at all, and neither is free wi-fi, for my understanding is that wi-fi is not a gravitational force. Perhaps it was a deliberate error to be spotted by a person with enough time on their hands to scrutinise it this closely. In which case, I was the chosen one.

The Days Inn chain was founded in the USA by Cecil B. Day, a devout Christian who offered the services of chaplains at his hotels, and complimentary Bibles for guests. Its logo is a blazing sun radiating spikes of light, as sometimes depicted behind Christ on the cross. In early Christian symbolism, Jesus was the spiritual sun, illuminating the world with divine insight. So perhaps it wasn't the fiery star to which the poster referred, but the word of God, spoken through the medium of a budget chain hotel, much as God spoke through his son, a humble carpenter. So perhaps this poster was trying to tell me that the promise of free wi-fi is what pulls people into the Days Inn in the same way that the Holy Spirit attracts the devout to the bosom of God. This insatiable desire for wi-fi is thanks to our compulsion to post crap on Facebook, check emails and watch Netflix, which is what I decided to go to my room and do.

||||||||||||||||

It was still dark the next morning when I checked out of the Days Inn and headed to Starbucks to get a coffee. Amid the parp and burp of the cafe's elevator jazz, two men in baseball caps talked in French while a businessman stared bleakly at half a croissant and a Spanish girl yattered on her phone. I took my scalding hot drink on a tour of the service station perimeter where a rotting wooden fence separated Corley Services from an adjacent field. In the distance I could make out the roofs of farmhouses beneath the brow of a wooded escarpment, shimmering in the mist like a motorway's fever dream of the land that came before it. Service station designers don't like their customers to be aware that the countryside is just a stone's throw away, in case they head out in search of pubs, shops, or wild camping, which is why they try to screen it with trees and fencing. When you are on the motorway, there is only the motorway and you must stay on that motorway with its motorway rules and motorway prices until a designated slip road releases you from the contract.

I finished my coffee while joining the slow procession of cars that I had left the previous evening. At the side of the road JCBs clawed at mounds of soil among freshly hacked woodland. It involved a great deal of environmental trauma to transform a dumb motorway into a smart one, mutating the highway into a cyborg fusion of tarmac and intelligent computer software, doomed to become aware of itself. Among the severed trees was a stump with two branches sticking out on either side like arms, dressed in a hi-vis vest and a hard hat, with a smiling face. Unsettled by this motorway golem, I cruised beneath the sinister sunflowers of average-speed cameras, the yellow agents of the motorway panopticon. They don't flash so you're never sure if they've caught you, or if they are even activated at all. There is rarely a speeding driver in an average-speed check area. Transgression is difficult when you assume that you're always being watched.

Eventually, the restrictions ended. The traffic flowed freely north of Birmingham as the motorway soared over warehouses, storage facilities and chimneys. To my right I passed a gigantic Travelodge which was once Fort Dunlop, a tyre factory built in the 1920s. Next to it was Fort Shopping Park, its chain-store brand names casting their glow onto the motorway before they fade into the grey tones of the Gravelly Industrial Park. The warehouse monoliths of IKEA, B&Q, Halfords and Currys led me through Walsall and Bloxwich, until I finally hit escape velocity and all around me was turned to fields.

At Hilton Park Services I parked by the perimeter, crudely barriered with corrugated-iron panels, hastily cobbled together as if to keep out a dangerous beast. The service-station building looked like an old hovercraft port, topped with a three-tiered glass tower, with transmitter antennae and masts poking from a top deck, serviced by steel access ladders. This was the intention in 1967 when it was built by the Rank Organisation, which created some of Britain's first services under the moniker Top Rank. It called them 'motorports', using futuristic architecture to create a distinctive brand, investing twice the amount recommended by the government in an attempt to dominate the industry. But like a twentieth-century Icarus, Top Rank flew too close to the motorway services sun. The company's ambition was its undoing. Its architectural aspirations were too expensive to construct and maintain; it was forced to cut back on its plans and finally quit the industry in the 1990s. Hilton Park's space port for cars remains a shabby relic of that utopian vision.

Inside the building, it seemed as if time had not moved for decades. I was assailed by 1990s house music and a stench of baked beans from the cafeteria. Its clothes shop displayed rows of tops with barely distinguishable differences set out on racks decorated with red balloons. At the counter, a woman in glasses held a phone to her ear and stared out across the empty floor. Beyond the usual takeaway food chains was the Lucky Coin fruit-machine zone and the ubiquitous coin-operated massage chairs, which I have never seen anybody use in any service station, ever. I entered a spacious stairwell with a hexagonal column of impressive girth in its centre, designed to take visitors up the tower, which originally housed a restaurant. I imagined all those people ascending these stairs in their tank tops, flares and corduroy, excited at the prospect of eating high above the dazzling new highway. Without them, and without the restaurant, there was an eeriness to this grandiose space, which now served only to provide access to the little-used pedestrian bridge. My footsteps sounded hollow in the corridors of a failed dream.

After Hilton Park came another restricted-speed zone, slowing the traffic once more into a steady crawl. Fog descended. Cows, farm buildings, church spires and the roofs of country houses emerged as disembodied entities in a white soup, fragments in a fantasy of old England, then receded slowly behind me, as if I was drifting along a river. It reminded me of how swans are sometimes fooled into landing on the wet tarmac, causing tailbacks as they waddle up and down, baffled by the unexpected solidity of the water.

As it turned out, my next stop, Stafford North Services, had a bird sanctuary. There was a lake with an ornamental fountain surrounded by a sloping green lawn and a sign informed me that the common reeds, rushes and sedge were home to dragonflies and damselflies, while blackbirds and swallows liked to visit for a drink or a bath. I couldn't see any of this wildlife, nor any human beings for that matter, but it was a weekday in early January and there was no reason for anyone to be here.

What I did find, beside the entrance of the main building, were three standing stones, covered in lichen, with facial features sculpted on them. The foremost had bulbous, terror-stricken eyes; its neighbour's eyes were closed, its mouth open as if in the midst of a desperate protestation; and the smaller stone behind them wore what looked like a death mask. There was no plaque to explain why they were there but I had a theory. Stafford North opened in 1996 and was a trailblazer in many ways: it was the first to eschew carpets in favour of polished wood floors; information boards were installed to enlighten visitors with details of things to see and do in the local area; and in the first few months, members of staff were positioned at the entrance to welcome visitors and hand out ashtrays, a personal touch intended to help the service station stand out from the competition. My theory is that when this dubious plan failed to make an impact, it was necessary to remove these workers quietly, to avoid bad press and legal recriminations for unfair dismissal. That was when a rogue station manager, ambitious for promotion and deeply into the occult, decided to take matters into his own hands. Summoning demonic forces, he cast a spell and turned the door staff into stone effigies on the spot where they stood, mouths open in surprise. They remain at their posts to this day, green with algae, blackened by exhaust fumes, staring out at the car park, sad monuments to a bad idea.

As I headed north from Stafford, the fog intensified, reducing the topography to an interplay of shadows, as if the world beyond the crash barriers was an illusion and the only reality was the road. I caught glimpses of strangely undulating hills – remnants of ancient earthworks, a Saxon fort, or a lost medieval village, woven with trackways hewn by hooves and feet.

When Staffordshire gave way to Cheshire, I entered what is considered to be the most haunted stretch of road in Britain, according to research commissioned by the construction company Tarmac. Supernatural phenomena have included a ghostly hitchhiker, a phantom truck driving in the wrong direction and Roman legionaries on the march. Tony Simmons, who worked on the survey, told the *Guardian*: 'We assumed Britain's spookiest road would turn out to be a dark lane near an ancient battlefield. But, when you think about it, these findings make sense. The M6 is one of Britain's longest roads and it travels through many counties – and therefore an immense amount of history.'[49] Mike Brooker, a psychic medium whose school friends were killed in a crash on the M6, calls the section of motorway between Junctions 16 and 19 'Cheshire's Bermuda Triangle' because of its unusually high number of accidents, which he believes are caused by vengeful ghosts, rudely woken by construction work. He told the *Daily Mail*: 'There appear to be two principal answers. One is that the motorway was built on a Roman burial site and the other is that it was the site of the slaughter of a Scottish army.'[50]

The M6 is not the only one to have churned up Roman history. Clacket Lane Services on the M25 is built on an old Roman road. Fragments of pottery found during the excavations are displayed in a cabinet between the gents' and ladies' toilets. Up at Scotch Corner, where the Leeming to Barton dual carriageway was expanded into a motorway in 2017, archaeologists discovered remains of a previously unknown town, which included a mixture of Roman and Iron Age buildings. The find was significant because it was evidence of how Queen Cartimandua of the tribal Kingdom of Brigantia collaborated with Roman invaders in the years before Britain was incorporated into the Empire. She manufactured Brigantian coins to trade with Romans and embraced their architecture. When a native Briton, Caratacus, fled from the Romans, seeking sanctuary in Brigantia, Cartimandua arrested him and gave him up in return for a reward, securing her place in Iron Age ignominy.

I took another pit stop in Sandbach, one of the service stations in the M6 Bermuda Triangle. I was captivated by the sight of its pedestrian footbridge, covered by a fire-engine-red canopy that stood independently of the buildings on either side. Inside, the paint was dark blue. Liquid pooled onto the concrete footway, and there was a pervasive oily smell, as if I was on an abandoned tanker. Peering through the smudged windowpane I could see McDonald's Golden Arches burning through the mist.

I wondered how many people had stood here in this same spot, looking at the lights of the traffic below over the past half a century. In the 1990s, it might have been someone high on ecstasy, head throbbing with the aftermath of loud techno, for Sandbach was one of a cluster of service stations that had a key role in northern underground dance culture. As Dan Slee, who grew up in Stafford, recalls:

> There were a handful of places where you could hear techno being played. The Hacienda in Manchester was one. Shelley's in Stoke-on-Trent was another. As word spread, people came from all over the country via the M6 to visit Shelley's. But at chucking-out time people were still buzzing. So, we'd head to the M6 and the service stations. Knutsford, Hilton Park and Sandbach. We'd pull into somewhere at 4 a.m. and the car park would be full of cars with windows down, playing techno with people dancing outside. The louder the better. Sometimes a bigger sound system arrived and a cheer would go up. The car park would turn into a techno version of *Fame*. Eventually, the police cottoned on and they coned off the car park. If you were a family driving through the night, you got in. If you were a car full of ravers playing breakbeats, you were told to clear off.

Motorways and music often go together. The M6 is a recurring motif in the songs of the Birkenhead rock band Half Man

Half Biscuit. Their track 'M-6-ster' is an oblique evocation of the motorway experience, in which the singer asks his dad the classic back-seat question, 'are we nearly there yet?', with references to Knutsford and the haulage company Norbert Dentressangle. Their video for 'Dickie Davie Eyes' was filmed in Forton Services, 'Our Tune' mentions Hilton Park and 'Ode to Joyce' references Tebay. Mark E. Smith rails against the M5 on The Fall's album *Middle Class Revolt*, in which the motorway makes work for idle hands in rush hour as people try to escape from the city to an agrarian ideal. Likewise, Chris Rea's 'Road to Hell' is about being trapped on the M25 orbital, a river that does not flow. More positively, Black Box Recorder's 'The English Motorway System' describes these roads as beautiful and strange entities, while The Tom Robinson Band's '2-4-6-8 Motorway' is inspired by the singer's memories of driving back from gigs down the M1 as the sun came up.

Like the M6, the M1 brought about dramatic transformation to Britain by joining the north and south in a high-speed corridor that was considered the new Great North Road. Opened in 1959, it has its own musical document in the radio folk ballad, *Song of a Road*, recorded by Ewan MacColl, Charles Parker and Peggy Seeger, and broadcast on the BBC Home Service that same year. Along with American Alan Lomax, MacColl was part of a folklore revival in the 1950s that sought to incorporate the contemporary working-class experience into a new form of urban pastoral. For the creation of *Song of a Road* he and the production team were given access to the construction site of the M1, then known as the London–Yorkshire Motorway, where they recorded the sounds of diggers, earth-movers, drills, pouring concrete and aggregate, and interviewed the workers, including immigrants from Ireland, the West Indies, Pakistan, Greece, Africa, Poland and Turkey. In one segment, a workman explains that he is fascinated by the resemblance of earth-moving machines to prehistoric monsters, digging up fragments of earth that are millions of years old. The mythic quality of these observations is blended with songs of roaming ramblers and sand-shifter shanties, which serve to connect the building of the motorway to the shipyards and railways of the nineteenth century.

As I continued on my journey up the M6, I thought about what a sight those first stretches of must have been in the 1950s – a long corridor of giant earthworks scything through the countryside. Unofficial Britain reader Damian Morley, whose family was local to that area, recounts his first ever glimpse, aged seven: 'I spent a few days with my aunt, uncle and cousins in the outskirts of Preston. I could hear machinery working in the distance all night. My cousin took me through a bluebell wood to look. They were building the Preston Bypass, the first part of the M6.'

I imagine that young boy in Lancashire as a member of a remote Amazonian tribe, parting the leafy jungle foliage to behold the trucks and chainsaws of the loggers for the very first time, unfamiliar technologies that are about to change his way of life forever. He just can't comprehend it yet.

||||||||||||||||

When motorways first appeared, they were thrilling enough to be depicted on postcards. Some are collected in the artist Martin Parr's book *Boring Postcards*, described as 'a record of a folk photography', depicting airports, underpasses, hospitals, housing estates and shopping precincts in images taken between the 1950s and 1970s. The collection kicks off with motorway scenes: the nascent M1 in monochrome, with sharp lines and freshly grassed verges; the M6 in lurid greens and oranges, with crisp white lines to mark the lanes; the service stations of Corley, Keele and Charnock Richard with their futuristic restaurant bridges – sun-soaked concrete beneath blue skies; interior shots of businessmen in suits and thick glasses at Formica tables in elegant lounges with brown carpets. Despite the title of his collection, Parr is aware that these photographs of 'non-places' are anything but dull because their utopian visions of motorway life contrast amusingly with our reality in the twenty-first century. It is not the postcards in Parr's book that are intrinsically boring, but we ourselves who have become bored, thanks to the twin passion-killers of familiarity and disappointment.

The vision of motoring freedom on luxurious superhighways never quite transpired. The motorway has become weighted with experience. Congestion. Tailbacks. Horrific accidents. Overpriced food in dilapidated restaurants. The images in *Boring Postcards* are relatively recent – many people over fifty years old might recall similar-looking motorways and service stations – but they also seem hugely historical. They represent a time of innocence, before we understood the implications of our oil addiction for the world's climate and ecosystems, or that no matter how many motorways we created, they would always fill up.

We are almost as many years on from Parr's book, published in 1999, as he was from the later examples in his collection. Since then we've experienced huge transformations and upheavals, from the explosion of the internet revolution, with its limitless virtual landscapes, to the acceleration of global warming and the coronavirus pandemic. But while we have changed in many ways, the motorway remains comfortingly constant, which is perhaps why some of its features have become cherished landmarks.

The final motorway postcard in Parr's book depicts Forton, now known as Lancaster South service station, the jewel in the M6 crown and one of the most famous sights on the motorway. In the 1960s, Top Rank recruited T.P. Bennett & Son to construct a magnificent twenty-metre tower. Topped with a hexagonal, cantilevered double-decker platform, it was designed to house a restaurant in the sky from which diners could gaze over the North Lancashire plain and Bowland Fells. It was known as the Pennine Tower and, in its heyday, was visited by celebrities including the Beatles, but it was too costly to run successfully and its single fire escape was deemed unacceptable for new health and safety regulations, so the owners decided to close it.

There is a rumour that the real reason the restaurant was shut down is that the hexagonal platform looked like a UFO when lit up at night, panicking drivers on the motorway who had never seen it before. When I stopped for a break there during my fateful journey with Jason in 1999, I remember being struck by the tower's *Close Encounters* effect as it hovered above sodium lights in a shroud of mizzle. I cannot recall any specifics such as where we sat or what we said, only the alien structure looking over me and the feeling of the hot coffee cup against my fingertips. So many memories are like that. Sensations rather than pictures. Forcing us to fill in the missing visual details and dialogue, rendering them as fictions based on truths. The older I get the more I realise that the past is as unknowable as the future; it is just as prone to supposition and speculation.

Arriving now, a man in his mid-forties who had taken it upon himself to drive up the M6 for no reason at all – something the young me would have found baffling – I was not especially interested in the Pennine Tower. Perhaps it had featured in too many postcards. Too many blogs. Too many Instagram posts. Instead, I snuffled around the side of the building, seeking out the unofficial story on the ground level, where I was immediately intrigued by a Portakabin with wire mesh strung across its windows and a sign bearing the ancient term FAX MACHINE above the door.

Brian Crompton has sold and repaired CB radio equipment from this little prefab building for twenty years, but has actually been on site since Valentine's Day 1990 when he began selling his products from a repurposed bus that he would drive to Forton every day. Brian is one of those quietly legendary figures who become an intrinsic part of a place, not because of any particularly unique talent or action, but through the sheer persistence of their presence over time. People like Victoria Hughes, who ran the public toilet facilities on the Downs in Bristol between 1929 and 1962. Her customers were predominantly sex workers, so she would offer them hot tea, financial help and advice. Now she is commemorated by a blue plaque that remains on the toilets to this day. Or more recently in Croydon, Harry Okaine, a Ghanaian man known locally as Prince Harry, who sat every day at a junction on Purley Way, in sunglasses and a floppy hat, to advertise the nearby scrapyard. These eccentrics are heroes of the everyday, becoming so ingrained in a place that it is impossible to imagine it without them, and their eventual disappearance is as traumatic as ravens leaving the Tower of London.

The rear of the services building was like a decayed 1960s office block serviced by a steel staircase, surrounded by bins, paint pots, rat traps, a rotting picnic bench and an open shipping container full of cardboard. Beyond the HGV filling station, the perimeter was a bordered by boggy grass, raised earth and briars. As I squelched my way around it, I encountered a padlocked enclosure of wire fencing set between heavy-duty wooden posts. Inside were two rectangular concrete blocks, standing parallel to each other about two metres apart, and off to the side a third block of concrete formed in the shape of steps. They were all covered in moss. Strewn on the dead leaves around them were chocolate-bar wrappers, Styrofoam cups, and crisp packets, bleached almost white by the sun. There were sharp barbs on the top of the fence making it very clear that people were not supposed to enter the enclosure. By why would someone want to? What was this Concrete Henge and what did it mean?

I could not work out if it was an aborted structure that needed protection from the public or a toxic horror from which the public needed protection. Or perhaps this was a fully formed structure, looking exactly the way it was intended,

Concrete Henge.

surrounded by non-biodegradable plastic offerings, created by a secret ritualistic motorway subculture operating behind the distracting veneer of the Pennine Tower. Whatever the truth, Concrete Henge appears to have been here a long time, perhaps before Brian and his CB radios, and even the services itself.

At the edge of the Travelodge car park, a path cut through a mud bank and onto a winding lane that ran alongside a field of sheep and telegraph poles, towards some stone buildings with slate roofs in the distance. The membrane between motorway and the countryside was remarkably thin here. In a few steps I'd crossed a threshold and departed the universe of the M6 entirely. A hatchback tootled merrily past, the driver giving me a wave before he disappeared around the bend, back into the 1950s. For a while, I sauntered down the lane, crunching on fallen leaves, savouring the aroma of cow shit. Part of me wanted to keep going deeper into the countryside, until the services were no longer visible, crossing the fields into the woods, there to start a new life in this parallel universe, unchained from the shackles of the twenty-first century, leaving my car as the only clue to my disappearance. 'AUTHOR VANISHES FROM ICONIC SERVICE STATION', the headline would read, with a picture of the Pennine Tower instead of my face, because, of course, it's the tower with its UFO stylings and aborted sky restaurant that always gets the clicks, likes and shares. Only the tower would have endowed my story with vigour and meaning.

After my transgressive walk in the countryside I returned to the services and crossed the footbridge, where there were yet more 'caution wet floor' signs on a dry floor. Having seen this so many times, I now believed that there was no storeroom for these signs; instead they were cast like runes to stand in dry places in anticipation of future spillages and mop-ups. At the end of the footbridge I stopped outside a door with a sign: MULTIFAITH ROOM. A place for worship and divine contemplation above the M6. You might not always find a wet floor beneath a wet floor sign at Forton Services, but you can always find God.

‖‖‖‖‖‖‖‖‖‖‖‖

As the industrial North West gave way to rural Cumbria, the traffic thinned, allowing me to drive at full pelt on cruise control. By this point in the journey I had become fully tuned into the dialogue of cars as they jostled for position in the ever-evolving pecking order of the motorway. While there could be no direct conversation, there was plenty of physical communication between vehicles. Some drivers took offence when a seemingly lesser car made a move to overtake them, accelerating to prevent the humiliation and put the interloper back in its place. Others passive-aggressively admonished those who hogged the middle lane by making a blatant show of undertaking them on the empty inside lane, then swinging out in front of them again. Then there were the mavericks who opted to stay in the fast lane, no matter what, even with a queue of cars behind them. These are the self-elected moral guardians of the motorway, determined to convey the message that 70 miles per hour is the legal limit and anyone who wishes to bully their way past them is breaking the law. Their sworn enemies are the tailgaters, outside-lane speed freaks in expensive cars, or inexplicably high-powered white vans, almost always men, whose aim is to drive at the fastest the engine will go, at all times, for reasons related most likely to sexual inadequacies. Or at least that's what I muttered under my breath as I gave way to them. A motorway is a channel of repressed rage, jealousy and social politics, expressed in a ballet of metal machines moving at lethal speeds.

At signs for the Lakes, the fog cleared, revealing the foothills of a distant mountain, on which the blades of wind turbines turned and pylons were linked together like climbers on a difficult ascent. I was still on the same three lanes of tarmac that I'd been on all day, but the experience couldn't have felt more different. There were no Aldi, Big Yellow Storage or B&Q stores. No retail parks or industrial estates. These had been replaced by the slate roofs, drystone walls and wooden barns of long-established farms. Crows flapped out from the crenellated towers of medieval churches and amassed in murders on telegraph poles. Smoke coiled from unseen bonfires. Trees on the hilltops were like old crones bent into the wind. On a bridge a tractor towing a silage trailer was silhouetted against the sky. I passed an old house hunkered in a field below the road, chimney puffing, its stone blackened as if scorched by fire, with a ramshackle garden of chopped wood and hunks of battered farm machinery. It looked like something out of a short story by supernatural-fiction writer Robert Aickman, a place where an unsuspecting visitor might seek shelter for the night, only to endure a terrifying ordeal at the mercy of unexplained forces.

Tearing along the motorway, I was captivated by the constantly shifting mountain vista; each slight bend in the road revealed new colours, textures and compositions. This effect is no accident. As Tom Fort describes in his book *The A303*, in the 1950s architects and horticulturists advised the government on the layout of new high-speed roads, including their 'alignment, curvature, the avoidance of parallelism and ugly angularity, the interplay of light and shadow, and appropriate planting'.[51] They wanted roads to 'flow' in graceful arcs between embankments of grass and native trees such as beech and ash. The aim was to create a series of unfolding views that would appeal to the subconscious mind of a driver in a speeding vehicle, keeping them visually stimulated but never distracted by exotic plants or garish hoardings. Landscape architect Geoffrey Jellicoe, who was a big influence on early motorway planning, encouraged designers to take inspiration from the landscape-painting tradition of eighteenth-century England. At that time, artists and tourists who strove for the picturesque used a popular tool called the Claude Glass, a convex mirror that gave the viewer a perfectly framed view of the landscape, with heightened texture and tones – much like an Instagram filter today. As the social historian Ken Worpole points out: 'The Claude Glass, once used to "frame" the perfect composition, was in the twentieth century replaced by the car window.'[52] So, far from being natural, the landscapes we see while driving are in fact a creation of our shifting perception while we're in motion on a superstructure carefully constructed to produce that effect. These vistas exist only because of the combustion engine and the motorway, which means that what many of us idealise as 'the countryside' is in fact a projection of twentieth-century technology.

As I passed Kendal, with the North Pennines to one side and the Lake District to the other, the southbound side of the motorway gradually dropped away, and the road curved in a majestic sweep around a mountain. A speeding train appeared to the left of me, then pulled ahead. I had a powerful urge to push on the accelerator pedal and follow, but I had to remind myself that I had no ultimate destination and there was little point in going nowhere quickly. I was here to be here. Driving just to drive. I had been stripped of the usual anticipation about who I would see, or where I would end up at the other end, which is what usually gives journeys their emotional charge. This thought made me lonely, momentarily, roaring over Shap's Fell towards Penrith with no kids in the back asking me silly questions and no smiling faces to look forward to. Unofficial Britain reader Jackie Bates recalls that her family would always shout 'SHAP!' as their car passed the sign for the village, a common ritual on family journeys when familiar landmarks appear. When I was a child we would all compete to be the first to see Glossop's Ferro Alloys chimney as we descended from the peaks. To this day, whenever I visit my parents in Amesbury, my daughters eagerly look out for the statue of The Ancestor outside the Solstice Park Services which takes us off the A303 to their house.

At the side of the motorway near Shap is one of the most interesting 'blink and you'll miss it' landmarks on the M6: two circles of granite stones, at a site that takes its name from a small stream nearby, which Norse settlers referred to as 'the spring of Gunnar' or Gunnerkeld. It is one of numerous pre-historical ceremonial sites on the northern leg of the motorway. On the outskirts of Penrith is Mayburgh Henge, a horseshoe earthwork constructed around a standing stone. About five hundred metres away is a site known as King Arthur's Round Table, a Neolithic circular earthwork surrounded by a ditch, which got its name in the seventeenth century during a revival of interest in the Arthurian legend, when the site was presumed to have been a jousting arena.

Blackpool-born musician and teacher Mark Williamson was nineteen when he wrote a pamphlet called *Man, Motorways and The Mother: Stone Circles Cairns and Henges Around the M6 from Tebay to Penrith*. 'I was obsessed with stone circles. My hero Julian Cope was writing a book about them and I wanted to get in on that action. I discovered there were a whole bunch of stone circles within spitting distance of the section of the M6 that runs up and over Shap Summit. I packed a tent and some food in my mum's Vauxhall Nova and set off.' For him, the proximity of the ceremonial stones and contemporary highway was not coincidental; they were connected across time in some way that he did not yet understand but yearned to discover. For the young Mark, this most northerly reach of the M6 was no ordinary road, but a gateway to megalithic mysteries.

With the light fading, I reached the apex of the M6: Gretna Green, famed since the mid eighteenth century as a destination for eloping lovers, who were not permitted in England to marry before the age of twenty-one without parental consent. In Scotland, all it required was a declaration of your freedom to marry, and a few witnesses, so in the Blacksmiths Shop an 'Anvil Priest' carried out the ceremony for a fee. I exited the interchange in a matrimonial loop, becoming symbolically wedded to the M6, and rolled back onto the southbound carriageway to drive the short distance to Tebay South, the UK's only independent service station. Established by farmers John and Barbara Dunning in 1972 the southbound side started as a picnic area but was developed into a full-blown service station in 1993, mimicking the rural architectural style of its northbound predecessor: drystone walls, wooden beams and pitched roofs with low eaves.

The farm shop sold gourmet chocolates, meats, cheese and wine, while the restaurant walls were lined with historical local photographs; a steam train chugging through the Lune Valley; a woman carrying a sheep on her back; cows milked by hand; geese waddling through a village. Tebay was designed to look like a slice of authentic rural Cumbria that existed before the M6, preserved in the modern era, even though it came after the motorway and was equally complicit in the displacement of the countryside there before it.

In a raised area beside the overflow car park was a cluster of standing stones and an array of flat stones for picnicking. I sat on one of them, savouring the bright moonlight for a while and listening to the whoosh of cars behind the hill. Where had these stones come from? Were they here in the landscape already or transported on trucks to tie the service station to the narrative of the ancient world? Did it matter? What was the difference between a 5,000-year-old standing stone and the overflow car park of a motorway service station? Only the passing of time made one more special than the other. For all I knew, the stone circles of Gunnerkeld and Mayburgh were the relics of service stations for travellers long gone, who once

Standing stones in Tebay South.

sat as I did, staring up at the moon on a cold night, wondering where it all began.

It was a good question. Where had my journey really started? Which event had led me to this moment beside the motorway? Perhaps it was the invention of the combustion engine, which simultaneously invented the modern carscape; the advent of mechanised weaving, which gave birth to the Industrial Revolution; or the hunter gatherer who first decided to farm a crop, creating the first permanent settlements, the first trade routes and eventually the first roads. The tale of these isles extends back to a time we cannot see and can only imagine. There is no true origin to the story of Britain and no foreseeable end to it. But here is where, arbitrarily, I decided to finish my account. My journey up the M6 had taken me from the factories and trading estates of the industrial Midlands, through futuristic motor ports and former rave-scene haunts to these standing stones in a motorway service station in the Cumbrian fells without leaving the same strip of tarmac. Almost all of the features I've written about in this book were visible on the route, jumbled across a myriad different topographies, but the motorway had arranged them into a neat, linear narrative, in the same way that we try to order the chaos of existence into a coherent story. Or as Jack Kerouac famously phrased it, 'The road is life.'

Come, follow, follow me
To the mountains of the north go we
Leave all that is behind forever
And let us go together
In the communion of the drive
Wherein we feel our most alive

At service stations we stop for respite
There with the Sun of God to spend the night
Days in, days out, we go
To places we used to love and know
The techno rave at night that blared
The dance on tarmac that we shared

Whatever aims we do intend
The motorway comes to an end
Its future dreams decayed
Its traffic by congestion stayed
But the ghosts don't stop their locomotion
Nor impede we travellers in our devotion

EPILOGUE

After a long trudge beside a ring road, you arrive at the crest of a flyover and pause for breath by a lamp post where flowers have been tied and initials inked onto steel by others who have stood here before you. Lovers. Friends. Mourners. Local kids say that you can sometimes see the ghosts of those who have jumped from here to their deaths, but perhaps that's a myth to keep folk away from the underpass, where they like to party after dark, daubing the walls in charms and sigils. A pigeon flaps out from a distant multistorey car park from which you can hear the revving of an engine, even though there has been no access to that car park for years. With a shiver, you descend a pedestrian footpath alongside a trading estate. You hear a hammer pounding on metal to the strains of a 1980s pop hit on FM radio. Someone shouts a name that sounds like yours. It grows cold and you don't know why, but you've heard stories about this place: a notorious car dealer who vanished without trace, a kid savaged by a dog – though some say it looked more like a wolfman. You hurry down a terraced street where a poltergeist is once said to have chased a distressed family from their council house. Beyond the roofs, pylons lead to a distant escarpment where a motorway stretches away beneath a halo of electric light. The shriek of a car alarm startles a crow from its perch on a TV aerial. Night is falling. You wonder about this strange place, and what will happen next.

||||||||||||||||

To put this book together, I roamed the streets in search of stories that would tell me something about the lore of everyday urban life. I travelled to the cities of Bristol, Glasgow, Hull, Manchester, Birmingham and London. I wandered the towns of Harlow, Northampton, Grimsby, Port Talbot, Greenock and Glenrothes. I revisited the places of my youth in Kirkintilloch, Wrexham, Glossop, Sheffield and Hackney. I drove on dual carriageways, ring roads and motorways. I parked in multistoreys and I slept in hotel chains. I delved into my childhood recollections and family history. What I learned on this journey is that everything changes and yet little does. Landscapes overlay landscapes, in ever-turning cycles. The flyover where a viaduct once stood. The Victorian workhouse that became a hospital. The steelworks on the site of a monastery. The burial cairn surrounded by a busy interchange. Motorway earthworks that rise alongside their Bronze Age predecessors. The pretty bend on the river that became a dirty dockland then a ramshackle trading estate then an artist's hub then an estate of luxury waterside highrises. After each new manifestation replaces the old, it too becomes worn, decayed and saturated with nostalgia, to the point where some mourn its passing as much as others once lamented its coming. So the circle turns.

The past is never absolutely destroyed but recycled into mutant strains. It seeps through the layers of a place and takes on new guises to give us goose-bumps and chills. Witches, ghosts and demons have not been entirely banished to legend – they haunt our homes, shops, hospitals and roads. The churches, forbidden woods and haunted mansions that were once the stuff of our dreams and nightmares have now been replaced in our imaginations by industrial estates, power stations and factories. Underpasses are our holloways. Pylons, chimneys and masts our landmarks. Motorways our great causeways. Roundabouts our stone circles. Multistoreys our crumbling castles. They can be as full of melancholy, magic and mystery as what came before, if you take time to get close to them and open your mind.

As I completed the final draft of this book, a lethal pandemic swept across the globe, the like of which we hadn't seen since 1918. Shops, pubs and schools closed down. Streets fell silent. Car parks emptied. Playgrounds were locked. Shoppers queued outside supermarkets with masks over their faces. Fruit went unpicked. People died in overwhelmed hospital wards without their loved ones being able to touch them. Within a few devastating months, life changed completely. What we had taken for granted was swept away with remarkable speed. The construct of our modern capitalist society was shown to be as flimsy as gossamer. Our physical interconnectivity changed from a blessing to a curse. Motorways, hotels and airports became conduits for disease. Food supplies suddenly looked tenuous as the supermarket shelves emptied, toilet rolls and dried pasta becoming prized rarities. Some reacted by reverting to feverish superstition, wrapped up in the guise of new urban myths, as they attacked mobile-phone masts in the belief that 5G technology was responsible for the coronavirus. It was like a scene from *The Changes*, which I discussed in the first chapter of this book. Stories spread that the virus was leaked from a high-security lab in Wuhan, China. David Icke proclaimed that the global lockdown was really a big push for control from the New World Order. Proponents of Gaia theory proclaimed that the planet's immune system was fighting back against its own pandemic – the human virus. We were the disease, they said. In the same way that Victorians reacted to the perceived threats of advancing technology, social shifts and globalisation by inventing stories of vampires and alien invaders, so too are we creating new monsters in this era of climate change, ecological disruption and global power shifts. As usual the monsters will turn out to be us.

The pandemic might have helped draw a starker line under the 'modern' landscape of the late twentieth century, and pushed it more rapidly into history, than I envisioned when I started writing this book. That near-past is now cast in a mythic haze as something of a lost world, haunting our collective memory, just like the pre-industrialised Britain of popular imagination. Whatever happens, nothing will return quite to the way it was before. As we shift into a new era, we will still feel the need to tell stories of the places in our lives, embellishing them with our anxieties, hopes and fears for the future. But whatever changes come, let us never fall prey to the delusion of a halcyon past and convince ourselves that any single period of history is more authentic than another; that we can somehow freeze culture in time, or return to what has long passed. From Merrie Olde England, to the industrial heydays of Empire, to the post-war Swinging Sixties, to the here and now, and onto the uncertain world of tomorrow, the tale of these isles will continue until the final storyteller's dying breath.

ACKNOWLEDGEMENTS

Thanks for the walks and conversations . . .

Kirsty Otos, Craig Scott, Martin Fuller, Stuart Silver, Jane Samuels, Marc Renshaw, Bobby Seal, Mark Hollis, Nick Edwards, Clare Archibald, Jackie Cheffins and Rachel Stenhouse, Maxim Griffin, Murdo Eason.

Thanks for the contribution . . .

Mark Williamson, Rowena Macdonald, Damian Morley, Seán Vicary, Dan Slee, Jackie Bates, Keith Sands

Thanks to everyone whose work I have quoted or referenced . . .

Richard Mabey, Kenneth Brophy, David Southwell, Phil Smith, Alyson Hallett, May Miles Thomas, Owen Booth, Salena Godden, Gary Budden, Tom Chivers, Bob Fischer, Richard Littler, Olivia Laing, James Knight, Annie Muir, Nick Papadimitriou, Jo Underhill, Toby Ferris, John Rogers, MJ Steel Collins, John Grindrod, Will Wiles, The Lost Tales Podcast, Joe Sampson, Jag Betty, Paul Phillips, Chris Moar and Graeme Edmiston, James K. Beaton and Leo Bruges, Karen Evans, Paul Summers, Leigh Wright (Ephemeral Man), Nell Frizzell, Adam Scovell, Charles Christian, Andy Hokano, Robin Furman, Moira

Martingale, Stuart Wilson, Ken Worpole, Christopher Petit, Bill Drummond, Mark Leckey, Dr Martin Johnes, Dr Sam George, Dan Hancox, Daniel Maudlin and Marcel Vellinga, Dan Duggan, Martin Parr, Tom Fort.

Thanks to everyone else who has contributed to the Unofficial Britain website since 2014 . . .

Ben Thompson, Alex Cochrane, Kit Caless, Emma Bolland, Paul Case, Morticia, Joshua Alexander, Erkembode, George Sandison, Laura Harker, Eijls, Adam Smith, Natasha Zielazinski, Owen Davey, John Ledger, Eddie Procter, Rhia Parker, Tony Todd, Tina Richardson, Ben Austwick, B G Nichols, Matt Botwood, Paul Hawkins, Craig Johnson, Jo Dacombe, Dave Fleet, Michael Hampton, David Hoffman.

Last but not least . . .

Thanks to Lee Humphries at Printed Matter, Hastings, for the books. To Emma and Jim Welch for the dog care. To Carolynne and Edward Donnelly for the accommodation. To Mum and Dad for the babysitting. Finally, to Simon, Pippa and Sarah for the faith and feedback.

BIBLIOGRAPHY

Books

Auge, Marc, *Non-places: An Introduction to Supermodernity* (Verso Books, 2009)

Ballard, J. G., *Concrete Island* (Jonathan Cape, 1974)

Beckett, Andy and Roger Luckhurst, *The Disruption* (Circadian Press, 2017)

Beresford, Kevin, *Roundabouts of Great Britain* (New Holland Publishers, 2014)

Booth, Owen, *What We're Teaching Our Sons* (Fourth Estate, 2018)

Bradshaw, Ross (ed.), *Utopia* (Five Leaves Publications, 2012)

Budden, Gary and Kit Caless (eds), *Acquired for Development By . . .* (Influx Press, 2012)

Budden, Gary and Maxim Griffin, *The White Heron Beneath the Reactor* (2019)

Caless, Kit, *Spoon's Carpets* (Square Peg, 2016)

Chivers, Tom, *Flood Drain* (Annexe Press, 2014)

Christopher, John, *The White Mountains/The City of Gold and Lead / The Pool of Fire* (Puffin, 1967–68)

Cresswell, Tim, *On the Move* (Routledge, 2006)

Duggan, Dan, *Luxury of the Dispossessed* (Influx Press, 2015)

Duman, Alberto, Dan Hancox, Malcolm James and Anna Minton (eds), *Regeneration Songs: Sounds of Investment and Loss from East London* (Repeater, 2018)

Fisher, Mark, *The Weird and the Eerie* (Repeater, 2016)

Folklore, Myths and Legends Of Britain (The Reader's Digest Association, 1973)

Fort, Tom, *The A303: Highway to the Sun* (Simon & Schuster, 2012)

Furman, Robin and Moira Martingale, *Ghostbusters UK* (Robert Hale, 1991)

Godden, Salena, *Springfield Road* (Unbound, 2014)

Grindrod, John, *Concretopia* (Old Street, 2014)

Hallett, Alyson and Phil Smith, *Walking Stumbling Limping Falling* (Triarchy Press, 2017)

Hawkes, Jacquetta, *A Land* (The Cresset Press Ltd, 1951)

Hing, Richard, Grey Malkin, Stuart Silver and Andy Paciorek, *Folk Horror Revival: Urban Wyrd -2: Spirits of Place* (Wyrd Harvest Press, 2019)

Lang, Olivia, *To the River* (Canongate, 2011)

Mabey, Richard, *The Unofficial Countryside* (Collins, 1973)

Massey, Doreen, *For Space* (SAGE, 2005)

Maudlin, Daniel and Marcel Vellinga (eds), *Consuming Architecture* (Routledge, 2014)

Merriman, Peter, *Driving Spaces* (Blackwell Publishing, 2007)

Moore, Alan, *Jerusalem* (Knockabout Ltd, 2016)

Morrison, Kathryn A. and John Minnis, *Carscapes: The Motor Car, Architecture, and Landscape in England* (Yale University Press, 2012)

Papadimitriou, Nick, *Scarp* (Sceptre, 2012)

Parr, Martin, *Boring Postcards* (Phaidon Press, 1999)

Rees, Gareth E., *Car Park Life* (Influx Press, 2019)

Rees, Gareth E., *Marshland* (Influx Press, 2013)

Rees, Gareth E., *The Stone Tide* (Influx Press, 2018)

Richardson, Tina, *Walking Inside Out* (Rowman & Littlefield, 2015)

Smith, Phil, *Walking's New Movement* (Triarchy Press, 2015)

Vaneigem, Raoul, *The Revolution of Everyday Life* (Editions Gallimard, 1967)

Wallis, Clarrie, and Elsa Coustou (eds), *Mark Leckey: O' Magic Power of Bleakness* (Tate, 2019)

Watson, Paul, *England's Dark Dreaming* (The Lazarus Corporation, 2018)

Wiles, Will, *The Way Inn* (Fourth Estate, 2014)

Worpole, Ken and Jason Orton, *The New English Landscape* (Field Station/London, 2013)

Films and Television

Best Before Death – dir. Paul Duane, 2019

Catman – dir. Graeme Edmiston, written by Chris Moar

Catman's Greenock – dir. James K. Beaton, Leo Bruges

The Changes (TV mini-series) – dir. John Prowse, 1975

The Conjuring 2 – dir. James Wan, 2016

The Devil's Plantation – dir. May Miles Thomas, 2013

The Enfield Haunting (TV mini-series) – dir. Kristoffer Nyholm, 2015

Doctor Who (TV Series)

    Inferno (7 episodes) – dir. Douglas Camfield, 1970

    The Poison Sky – dir. Douglas Mackinnon, 2008

Govan Ghost Story (TV play) – dir. David Hayman, 1989

Lost But Not Forgotten (film series) – Episode 3 Living Under Spaghetti – Dir. Joe Sampson, 2017

New Town Utopia – dir. Christopher Ian Smith, 2017

Radio On – dir. Christopher Petit, 1979

When the Lights Went Out – dir. Pat Holden, 2012

Websites

Anatomy of Norbiton http://anatomyofnorbiton.org/

The Art of Mark Hollis https://hollisart.wordpress.com/

Brymbo Steelworks http://www.brymbosteelworks.com/

The Devil's Plantation https://www.devilsplantation.co.uk/

Folklore Thursday https://folklorethursday.com/
Ghostbox Records https://ghostbox.co.uk/
Hookland https://hookland.wordpress.com/
Jane Samuels https://www.jane-samuels.com/
Lost But Not Forgotten https://thelostbutnotforgottenseries.com/
The Lost Byway http://thelostbyway.com/
Marc Renshaw https://marcrenshaw.com/
Motorway Services Online https://motorwayservicesonline.co.uk/
Mythogography https://www.mythogeography.com/
Ode to Welbeck https://structuraleye.co.uk/ode-to-welbeck
Pathetic Motorways https://pathetic.org.uk/
Psychogeographic Review http://psychogeographicreview.com/
The Psychogeographical Commission http://www.psychetecture.
    com/
Pylon Appreciation Society https://www.pylons.org/
Pylon of the Month https://www.pylonofthemonth.org/
Scarfolk https://scarfolk.blogspot.com/
Sheffield Paranormal https://sheffieldparanormal.wordpress.com
Spooky Isles https://www.spookyisles.com/
The Unexplained Podcast http://www.unexplainedpodcast.com/
Unofficial Britain http://www.unofficialbritain.com/
The Urban Prehistorian https://theurbanprehistorian.wordpress.
    com/
Wyrd Daze https://wyrddaze.wordpress.com/

NOTES

1. Richard Mabey, *The Unofficial Countryside* (William Collins & Sons, 1973), p. 11

2. Gareth E. Rees, 'A Dream Life of Hackney Marshes', published in *Acquired for Development By . . .* (Influx Press, 2012)

3. 'Stocksbridge Bypass ghostly 'Ring o' Roses children' first up close sighting', Sheffield Paranormal, https://sheffieldparanormal.wordpress.com/2011/04/29/stocksbridge-bypass-haunting/

4. Ken Worpole and Jason Orton, *The New English Landscape* (Field Station/London, 2013)

5. From 'Pylon' by Annie Muir, http://time41poem.WordPress.com

6. Ludovic McL. Mann, 'Earliest Glasgow', https://www.cantab.net/users/michael.behrend/repubs/mann_eg/pages/earl_glas.html

7. Interview in Compulsion Online, http://www.compulsiononline.com/falbum14.htm

8. Dorota Bawolek, 'The Ring Road Hermit', BBC, 22 March 2007, http://www.bbc.co.uk/blackcountry/content/articles/2007/03/22/homeless_polish_feature.shtml

9. Kenneth Brophy, 'Hyperprehistory', The Urban Prehistorian, 31 March 2019, https://theurbanprehistorian.wordpress.com/2019/03/31/hyperprehistory/

10. Robin Furman and Moira Martingale, *Ghostbusters UK: A Casebook of Hauntings and Exorcisms* (Robert Hale, 1991), p. 132

11. ibid.

12. Mike Covell and Abby Ruston, '16 Very Haunted Halloween Locations in Grimsby', *Grimsby Telegraph*, 29 October 2017, https://www.grimsbytelegraph.co.uk/news/11-haunted-halloween-locations-grimsby-687630

13. Jacquetta Hawkes, *A Land* (The Cresset Press Ltd, 1951)

14. Furman and Martingale, *Ghostbusters UK*, p. 132

15. Phil Smith, *Walking's New Movement* (Triarchy Press, 2015), p. 57

16. M. J. Steel Collins, 'Why I love haunted Govan', Spooky Isles, https://www.spookyisles.com/why-i-love-haunted-govan/

17. Mark Fisher, *The Weird and the Eerie* (Repeater, 2016)

18. Stuart Wilson, 'Five Links Memories', https://www.youtube.com/watch?v=LJPk5PrgA8k

19. Gary Budden and Maxim Griffin, *The White Heron Beneath the Reactor* (2019)

20. 'On Landscape Ontology, An Interview with Graham Harman', Landscape Archipelago, https://landscapearchipelago.wordpress.com/2012/07/01/on-landscape-ontology-an-interview-with-graham-harman/

21. J. G. Ballard, *Concrete Island* (Jonathan Cape, 1974)

22. *Bristol Evening Post,* September 1967

23. Salena Godden, *Springfield Road* (Unbound, 2014), p. 11

24. Elsa Coustou's interview with Mark Leckey in *Mark Leckey: O' Magic Power of Bleakness* (Tate, 2019), p. 15

25. Dr Martin Johnes, 'Welsh History Month: The M4 in South Wales', Wales Online, 9 April 2012, https://www.walesonline.co.uk/news/wales-news/welsh-history-month-m4-south-2047338

26. 'The "sweet little Chiswick Flyover" hits 50', *Evening Standard*, 1 October 2009, https://www.standard.co.uk/lifestyle/the-sweet-little-chiswick-flyover-hits-50-6746158.html

27. https://www.facebook.com/CatmanGreenock2

28. Olivia Laing, *To The River* (Canongate, 2011)

29. *Huffington Post,* 16 May 2016, https://www.huffingtonpost.co.uk/entry/8ft-tall-werewolf-old-stinker-prowling-in-hull-industrial-estate_uk

30. Dr Sam George, quoted in 'Why collective guilt may have fuelled sightings of the Old Stinker', *Yorkshire Post*, 22 October 2016

31. Jessica Haworth and Mark Branagan, 'Mystery "werewolf" creature terrifying families in Hull sparks major hunt', *Mirror*, 16 May 2016, https://www.mirror.co.uk/news/weird-news/mystery-werewolf-creature-terrifying-families-7979525

32. Tom Chivers, *Flood Drain* (Annexe Press, 2014)

33. Ian Thomson, 'Steamy Encounters', *The Spectator*, 20 January 2018

34. Alberto Duman, Dan Hancox, Malcolm James and Anna Minton (eds), *Regeneration Songs: Sounds of Investment and Loss from East London* (Repeater, 2018)

35. Matt Precey and Laurence Cawley, 'Inside Harlow's office block "human warehouse" housing', BBC, 3 April 2019, https://www.bbc.co.uk/news/uk-england-essex-47720887

36. John Grindrod, *Concretopia* (Old Street Publishing, 2013)

37. According to the Paranormal Database, https://www.paranormaldatabase.com/hotspots/glasgow.php

38. Sam Webb, 'Paranormal Parking', *Sun*, 4 May 2017, https://www.thesun.co.uk/news/3476365/chilling-cctv-footage-shows-supernatural-woman-at-car-park-disappear-into-solid-wall/

39. Jag Betty, 'The Haunting of Bell Street', https://www.youtube.com/watch?v=52pj2L90fSM

40. Jag Betty, 'Ghost Hunting at Bell Street Car Park, Dundee', https://www.youtube.com/watch?v=s6pxZfoAlTA

41. Clare Archibald, 'Contraflow', published on Walkingheads.net, http://www.walkingheads.net/contraflow-clare-archibald/

42. Owen Booth, *What We're Teaching Our Sons* (Fourth Estate, 2018)

43. Alyson Hallett and Phil Smith, *Walking Stumbling Limping Falling: A Conversation* (Triarchy Press, 2017)

44. Dan Duggan, 'A Sentence', *Luxury of the Dispossessed* (Influx Press, 2015)

45. Toby Ferris, 'Anatomical', Anatomy of Norbiton, http://anatomyof norbiton.org/anatomical.html

46. Alan Moore, *Jerusalem* (Knockabout, 2018), p. 825

47. Kathryn A. Morrison and John Minnis, *Carscapes: The Motor Car, Architecture, and Landscape in England* (Yale University Press, 2012)

48. Nell Frizzell, 'I Spent 24 Hours at That Motorway Wetherspoons', *Vice*, 2 October 2007, https://www.vice.com/en_uk/article/9k3zmv/i-spent-24-hours-at-that-motorway-wetherspoons

49. Martin Wainwright, 'Roman soldiers march on M6, Britain's most haunted road', *Guardian*, 31 October 2006, https://www.theguardian.com/uk/2006/oct/31/britishidentity.martinwainwright

50. Charlie Moore, 'M6 fatal crashes are due to ghosts including phantom lorries, vanishing hitchhikers and even Roman soldiers, says paranormal investigator', *Mail Online*, 23 September 2018, https://www.dailymail.co.uk/news/article-6198435/Psychic-claims-M6-haunted-crashes-caused-GHOSTS.html

51. Tom Fort, *The A303: Highway to the Sun* (Simon & Schuster, 2012)

52. Ken Worpole and Jason Orton, *The New English Landscape* (Field Station/London, 2013)

INDEX